Other Books by Karen L. Boncela

WORDS TO LOVE BY, 2012

ONE FATHER'S LOVE, 2013

Dark Secrets
No More

Karen L. Boncela

DARK SECRETS NO MORE by Karen L. Boncela

Copyright©2014 by Karen L. Boncela

Cover and interior designed by Ellie Searl, Publishista®

ISBN-13: 978-0615970486
ISBN-10: 0615970486
LCCN: 2014903012

Purple Knight Press
Naperville, IL

DEDICATION

This one's for you Eddie. Entirely.
I love you with every fiber of my being. Living with you has
enabled me to become the person I am now.
I never knew what I was capable of until you.
You gave me wings baby, and I thank you!

PREFACE

I FELT IT IMPERATIVE TO clarify my purpose for writing and publishing this book to my supportive readers as well as to those who may not be.

My intention has never been to belittle any person or find insignificant any disease. In fact my purpose is quite the opposite.

Alcohol and drug addiction of any kind is far from insignificant. Living with someone with the disease of addiction was life altering for me.

The purpose of this book first, is to share my personal story about overcoming adversity. Secondly, and just as importantly, I wanted to create a guide of sorts to help others out of similar heart breaking situations.

For thirty-two years my life revolved around my spouse. He demanded no less. I never had the privilege of putting my needs first. It was always about him.

Please let there be no mistake now.

This book is about me ... FINALLY ... ME!! This is the story of a huge part of MY life, MY struggle, MY awakening and MY triumph!

I have awakened in the middle of the night often, as I wrote this book and wondered if I was doing the right thing by sharing some of these disturbing memories. I've written some things in this book that I've never said out loud to anyone before. So many of the memories still make my heart pound.

I know in my heart though that this is the right thing for me to do for myself. I needed to write this story in order to finally put it to rest. It has been monumentally impactful on my whole life. It has created a large part of who I am.

I needed to write this courageously for the benefit of my readers as well. I wanted to be very clear about what it's like to live with someone who is a substance abuser. I remember for so many years just how alone I felt. I imagined that there could not possibly be anyone who was living the kind of life that I was. I couldn't possibly talk about what was going on in my home.

After I'd written *WORDS TO LOVE BY*, I realized that I needed to tell the rest of the story. I'd left out some very important parts about how I finally realized that I deserved to be happy and how I finally got the courage to do what I needed to in order to free myself . . . finally. So many of my readers have found *WORDS TO LOVE BY* so helpful and inspirational. I felt like I had no choice but to share the whole story.

I want to give hope to others who might be in a similar situation. I want to be specific in how I found my way into the light of happiness step by step. I want to give helpful tips in dealing with adversity. And in order to do all that and in order to tell the whole story honestly, I needed to include the facts of what happened whether they were ugly or not.

I believe that "*speaking the truth*" saved me. It saved my children as well.

CHAPTER 1

M Y MIND WAS SO FULL of anxious thoughts that I don't even know how I'd gotten to be just a couple of blocks away from the hospital, but I was suddenly jolted back into reality as I screeched on my brakes and drove up onto a curb to avoid running over a horrified pedestrian.

She screamed at me, "WHAT THE FUCK IS WRONG WITH YOU? WATCH WHERE YOU'RE GOING ASSHOLE!"

As she ran out of the crosswalk and onto the sidewalk, I realized that I should probably not have been behind the wheel at all in my mental state.

There were a lot of things then that I shouldn't have been doing but I felt I had no choice in the matter. As the woman ran away from me towards the hospital, I noticed only then that my face was wet with tears. She must have thought that I was crazy! I felt myself that I might be! My tears were of fear and horror of what my life had become.

I thought to myself, *How the hell did I get here? What kind of craziness is going on in my world?*

Pictures of my children popped into my head. I knew that I had to toughen up. I had to be okay for them. They really didn't have anyone else. I had to do what I had to do to get through this. I had a five year old son and two daughters that were two years old and just under one. They were counting on me to be there for them, for their everything. My children were my driving forces . . . they were what kept me going. Their existence was my reason for not giving up and for not throwing in the towel.

As soon as I collected myself enough to drive the car, I pulled into the parking lot and found a place to park. I wiped my face dry and as I walked into the hospital, I wondered what condition I would find David in. He had been pretty miserable the day before when I'd last left him.

I actually brought with me a briefcase that was full of paperwork from David's business. He owned a full service gas station back then and since he had been hospitalized, I was fooling myself and everyone else into thinking that I knew what I was doing to keep his business afloat when in reality, I didn't have a clue. I needed David's help in trying to figure out how I would get through the next day at his business. I needed him to show me how to do some of the paperwork and to tell me what to order, and how to handle the payroll there. It was an awful lot to expect from him in his condition, but I had no choice.

I'd been a stay at home mom for the past five years, and my husband David ran his business. At least I thought that's what he was doing. It was just in the last couple of weeks that I realized, without doubt, that David did not have his life or his business together at all. Everything about it was actually crumbling down around us one piece at a time. The life that I thought I'd known was a sham. I felt so betrayed and scared and stupid for not recognizing what was happening.

But I was so busy with the kids. I felt like a single mom. I did everything for them. I had no help. My mom had died way before her time and I didn't feel comfortable having my mother-in-law around. She was bossy and tried telling me what to do all the time. None of that mattered really, because she didn't make any offers to help me anyway.

I'd trusted that David was doing the right things and that he would take care of us financially if I did everything else. I'd been totally wrong in trusting him. This was becoming very apparent now with every new day. It was like I'd had blinders on. My focus was always my children.

As I walked through the front door of the hospital and into the lobby, the volunteer at the front desk greeted me with a smile and a question, "Can I help you find your way?"

"No thanks," I said. "I know where I'm going," which was a funny thing for me to say, because I felt so lost and alone.

I was so used to pretending that I was okay. I was accustomed to putting on a brave face when in fact, I would have liked to just crawl up into a ball and hide from the reality of my life.

I headed for the elevator and pushed the button for the third floor. I felt like I was in a daze. I felt like I must be living someone else's life. It was like an out of body experience. I was looking down at myself wondering what the hell I was doing here. It was the strangest feeling. It seemed like there had always been some kind of order to my life but now it felt like it was totally out of control.

As the elevator doors opened, I noticed there was still a small Christmas tree at the nurse's station. There were Christmas cards hung on the wall behind the nurses as they worked on their computers and chatted amongst themselves. They looked up at me and smiled as I passed by.

As I found my way to the family gathering room, I could hear the Christmas music being played. There were a few patients sitting on the couches with some family members but when I didn't see David in there, I walked to the room that he shared with three other men who were going through the same thing that he was.

They had all either checked themselves in, or had been forced to enter this program by family or the courts.

I could hear David speaking to his parents, as I walked into the room. David's voice sounded vulnerable and rather weak and defeated. It was such a stark contrast to his usual demeanor.

I heard his dad say, "What do you need to be here for? Are you so damn weak that you can't control yourself? You can't stop drinking on your own?"

"I need help, Dad."

David just kind of shook his head. He was used to the unkind and unsupportive words that normally came out of his father's mouth. I wondered why his father was even here.

As I walked into the room, Rita asked me "What have you got there, Karen?"

My mother-in-law was trying to change the subject, like usual . . . trying to ignore the ignorance of her husband's words . . . like always.

I put the briefcase down and then gave David a hug which he accepted warmly. I could feel his whole body shaking just a bit. His face was a bit bloated and red, all side effects I assumed of his body getting used to the absence of the alcohol and drugs that it was used to.

"Just some paperwork from the station that I need some help with," I said.

I really wanted to scream at Rita!

IF YOU AND YOUR HUSBAND CAN'T BE SUPPORTIVE HERE, JUST GET THE HELL OUT!

But I didn't.

I sat next to David as the three of them talked about unimportant drivel. His parents continued to tip toe around the elephant in the room.

As I looked at Rita, I remembered many conversations that we'd had about David's not so recent and disturbing behavior.

In one of our last conversations, I'd said to her, "Rita, he never comes home after work. He says he's out with the guys shooting pool and he crawls into bed late at night reeking of alcohol."

"Maybe he just needs to blow off some steam, Karen," Rita said.

"You're not getting it," I said, "he's doing this just about every night! I need help at home with the kids too! I can't do everything!"

"I'm sorry things aren't going well right now for you, Karen, but try to be patient with him. I'll see what I can find out," Rita had said.

I couldn't bring myself to tell her how bad things had become at home. I didn't tell her that more than once when he finally dragged himself home, he had a white powdery substance right on his nose! I thought if I just ignored what was becoming more and more apparent, that maybe it would go away.

I didn't tell her how mean and short tempered he had become. The kids and I had become afraid of him.

Because I had three small children, I had never been able to follow David around to find out what he was doing and where he was going. I realize now what a blessing that was. I wasn't about to get a babysitter to watch my children while I went out chasing David to see what he was up to, and I would have never packed the kids up in the car to do such a thing. I've realized that anything I'm meant to know in this lifetime will come to me with no effort on my part.

Rita had actually followed David to a bar after that last conversation, and was duped into believing that he was drinking a plain seltzer. Any admitted alcoholic/drug addict will confess honestly that they know how to manipulate the people around them in order for them to continue doing what they are doing. They know how to bullshit anyone, and David was full of it, no doubt.

She actually phoned me to say, "I think that you are totally wrong, Karen. I met up with David at the bar, and he was drinking just a soda. I had a good conversation with him and I believe that he was telling me the truth when he said that he is certainly not involved with drugs in any way."

Of course, Rita could not see David's behavior with me. He was a very good actor. For that matter so was I. David had everyone fooled into thinking that he was a nice guy. He saved his worst for me. My kids saw a bit of what David was really like but I bore the brunt of the majority of his outrageous behavior.

He only showed his true colors to me, and I believed that it was part of my job as his wife to cover up for him. I couldn't tell people who he really was. I couldn't tell them how mean he was to me. It was too embarrassing. I'd always hoped that my life with David would miraculously become peaceful and pleasant. I kept thinking if I loved him enough and if I supported him enough, things would be better between us. After all, our marriage vows had stated for better or for worse, and I thought if I could only tolerate the bad stuff for long enough there would be some kind of reward at the end.

I zoned out really as the three of them talked about nothing until they decided it was time to go home. Rita gave David a hug goodbye and the two of them left us alone. David's roommates were not in the room.

David stood then and hugged me, and as I clung to him he said, "I was in group therapy today . . . it made me realize some things. I've been such an ass to you and the kids. I'm so sorry."

"Wow, are you really?" I asked.

"Yes I am . . . and I want to make it up to all of you, especially you. I love you Karen."

He hugged me again and we both cried. It was like a floodgate of emotion just beginning to burst.

My first thought was, *Oh My God, he doesn't hate me!*

I had thought for so long that for a person to treat me the way that he had been, he must have hated me.

He'd been so mean, so many times. I remembered . . .

It was just a couple of days since I'd come home from the hospital after giving birth to my second child. I was sitting on the couch in the living room nursing Gina. My son J.R. had fallen asleep in his bedroom. It was nice and quiet. I was languishing in the moment and leaned my head back and closed my eyes to rest. I'd not had an easy delivery. Because of a failure to dilate, I'd ended up having a C-section delivery. It wasn't planned even though J.R. had also been born by the same method with the same issues leading up to it. I had switched doctors after J.R.'s birth to a doctor who would allow me to go through labor. I had felt like maybe the surgery was done too quickly the first time, and I wanted the chance to labor again to see if I could, in fact, have a normal delivery.

When my labor dragged on for most of a day without much progress, and the baby started to show signs of distress, it was decided by my two doctors that another C-section was probably the best course of action.

I can remember them leaning up against the wall near me, in the room where I labored. Both doctors and David were discussing the situation.

Dr. Halama said to Dr. Falcone, "I want to ensure the baby's safety as well as Karen's. I would suggest that we get her prepped for surgery immediately before the baby's stress worsens."

Dr. Falcone said, "I agree. Let's get this done quickly. David, would you like to be in the room at Karen's side?"

David said, "Yes, I would."

Both doctors looked to me for my permission. By this time I was exhausted and just wanted the pain to be over, so of course I agreed.

Both of the doctors reached their hands out to David to shake on the agreement to proceed.

David smiled as he said, "Thanks to both of you. You know, she's a really good mom, but she just isn't very good at this birthing thing, is she?"

I can still see the stunned looks on both of their faces. Can you even imagine? They must have both thought that he was a total moron.

Can I ever forget these things? I don't see how . . .

So as I rested there on the couch, I could hear David's voice. He'd been lying down next to J.R. I had assumed he was napping as well but that was not the case. It sounded like he was on the phone with someone.

I got up and laid the baby down in her bassinet in our bedroom.

David's voice got louder as I approached the bedroom. I didn't want him to wake J.R. As I crept into the room quietly, I could hear David's end of the conversation.

He said, "Oh fuck, I can't wait to get out of here. She's insisting that I stay here with her to help out. She's such a bitch!"

I opened the door quietly and nudged him.

I whispered, "I really need to rest. Can you get out of here so he will sleep for a while? You're talking too loudly."

David frowned and mumbled, "Yeah, whatever." He said on the phone, "I gotta go."

As he walked out of the room with me, I said, "Were you seriously just calling me a bitch? Who the hell were you talking to?"

He said, "One of my work buddies. I'm going to lie down. I'm tired too. I wasn't talking about you."

There was no question that he was referring to me but I just shook my head wearily and said, "I'm going to lie down in the bedroom with the baby. Please lay on the couch for now, okay?"

He said, "Okay."

It was such a huge relief now, first and foremost that maybe, just maybe he still loved me. This was after all, the first time in I don't know how long, that David was free of alcohol and drugs for a full week. I was hopeful that he may have been starting to think more clearly than he had in a while.

"They actually want you to come to some therapy groups . . . there will be other family members there as well," David said.

"I'm willing to do whatever it takes to make us a happy family again. Who else will be coming to therapy with us?"

David said, "I've asked my parents to attend. I didn't get a very good response from my father but I think that my mother may go along with it."

"Well that's good to hear. I'll do whatever they suggest to help you and to help us as a family. How are you feeling today anyway?"

"I feel like fucking shit! I can't sleep. I had the sweats all fucking night and I can't stop my hands from fucking shaking. But I have to get past all this before I will feel better. The counselors here seem pretty helpful. I think I can relate to some of them. Some of them are recovering addicts themselves. They've told me that all the fucking symptoms I'm having are normal so I just have to get through this."

"You can do this," I said. "You have to. The kids and I need you."

"I'm going to try," David said.

As we hugged again, my eyes welled with tears as I thought for the first time in a long time that maybe we could fix this. Maybe we could repair this marriage of ours. I hoped that this program would help David and me, and our kids become a healthy family again. As I say that now, I realize that we probably never were a healthy family. It was kind of warped from the very beginning.

"Let's take a walk and see what's going on in the family room," I said. "We can look at some of this paperwork afterwards, ok?"

"Sure," he said.

As we walked down the hall we could hear the sounds of voices and music coming from the family room. It was full now of patients and their families. It was Sunday and Sunday was a big family visiting day. Patients were allowed to take it easy on this day, to visit with friends and family.

There were patients of many ages; men and women alike. There was a pool table in the middle of the room and a large screen TV at one end. Couches and chairs filled up the other walls.

"Hey David, how are you today? And is this Mrs. David?" asked one of the nurses who was attending to one of the male patients who was sitting in a wheelchair with an IV bag hanging next to him.

David said, "I'm doing ok, and yes this is my wife, Karen."

"Nice to meet you Karen," said the nurse.

"Nice to meet you as well," I said.

We found a spot to sit down on the couch and as we looked around, David started describing to me some of the people we were looking at. He seemed to take comfort in the fact that they were all sharing similar experiences.

I guess we all take comfort in knowing that there's always someone else whose struggles are even worse than our own.

"That's Martin over there. He had to come into treatment. His only other choice was jail time."

"Wow!" I said. "That would be really tough for a guy his age, don't you think?"

"How old do you think he is?" David asked.

"Maybe sixty?"

"He's only forty five but he's been living a pretty rough life," David said.

"Oh my gosh," I said.

As I looked over at Martin it was plain to see he had some issues. As he spoke to what looked like his wife, he waved to David from across the room to say hello, and as he did I could see that his hands were shaking visibly. His face looked swollen, and his skin seemed visibly yellow. His hair was about fifty percent gray.

As David waved back, he said in a low voice, "Charles is the name of the guy over there in the wheelchair. He's about fifty years old and I heard him tell his story. His estranged wife found him on the floor of his kitchen after no one had heard from him in several days. He had admitted to drinking for several days non-stop and couldn't really remember how long he'd been lying on the floor there. He's in pretty bad shape."

"Will he be okay?" I asked.

David said, "I don't know. He says they are running lots of tests on him to see what they can do to repair all the problems he's having from the alcohol abuse."

I couldn't help the tears welling up in my eyes as I heard these stories. I thought to myself that surely, we had gotten David here just in time. He'd been heading on the same course of self-destruction at thirty years old.

Almost panicked I said, "David, that could be you in a few years, do you realize that? Is that what you want for yourself? For me? For the kids?"

I couldn't help but feeling really pissed off at this point that David would do this to himself! The realization of David's possible demise from what he'd been doing to himself hit me then, like I'd been knocked off the side of the Grand Canyon, screaming bloody murder all the way to the bottom!

How could he do this to us???

I was so relieved that he was in treatment but so pissed off that he had done this to himself, never seeming to think about what it would do to all the people around him, especially me and the kids.

"Of course, I don't want that!" David said through clenched teeth, "That's why I fuckin agreed to come here!"

I felt so conflicted, feeling bad for him one moment and the next just wanting to kill him for messing up our lives! But like usual, I buried my own feelings for the sake of his.

I had to get away from him for a moment so I got up and walked over to the table on the other side of the room that was full of snacks and drinks that had been brought by all the patients' guests for sharing.

There was a middle aged woman who introduced herself to me. "I'm Carol. I'm a patient here as well. Are you David's wife?"

"Yes, I am," I said.

She laughed as she said, "He's a pretty good volleyball player."

"Really?"

"Yeah, a group of us were playing yesterday and he smacked the ball over the net and hit me in the head so hard I saw stars!"

"Oh," was all I could say as I walked away with my drink back to David.

I couldn't help it. The anger in me just welled as I thought of everything I had to take care of at home. I had to do everything for the kids and David's business while he was here, having his meals served to him, playing volleyball, one on one counseling, and exercise. It just didn't seem fair! I was just as big a mess as him emotionally, probably more so! There was no question really . . . I was a wreck.

It didn't seem to matter though.

"David, let's go back to your room so that we can look at some of this paperwork from the station that you need to help me with, ok?" I asked as calmly as I could.

Keep it together Karen. Just a little longer and I can get out to the car and scream!

As we walked back, all the thoughts inside my head were jumbled up so badly that I could hardly think. When we got back into his room, I picked up the briefcase that I'd left there in his closet and handed it to David.

"I need you to help me make up the employee schedule for next week. And payday is coming up . . . you need to show me who gets how much. I also need help with ordering supplies."

"Okay, Okay! Slow the fuck down! Let me look at all this," he said.

I sighed, "Fine."

David tried to organize the papers inside the briefcase for a couple of minutes as I thought about what a joke it was really, that I was trying to run his business for him on top of everything else I was responsible for at home. I'd been a full time mom and had no time to become involved with the business. I had no idea what I was doing there, and I was hoping that David could fill in a lot of the blanks for me so that somehow, someway I could muddle through the next day.

As I looked across at him, I could see that he was getting frustrated as well. He was obviously having a difficult time thinking in his state of withdrawal. I would have loved to have gotten my answers from another reliable source, but there was none available to me and I wanted nothing more than to ensure that his business would be there for him after his rehab stay. It was our only source of income.

"So can you help me with the payroll?" I asked.

"Yeah, let me show you on paper how I do it," David said.

As he wrote down some figures on the pad of paper I'd handed to him, I could see how his hands were shaking, making the writing somewhat illegible.

"All right," I said, "and can you show me how you do the bank deposits?"

David looked inside the business check book that was in the briefcase and when he couldn't make out his own previous entries, he slammed it shut and threw it back into the briefcase and shouted, "I CAN'T FUCKING DO THIS NOW! WHAT THE FUCK DID YOU BRING ALL THIS TO ME FOR?"

"Because I have no choice! I don't know how to do any of this!" I pleaded as I began to cry. "I'm trying to keep your business going for you!"

"YOU CAN TAKE ALL OF THIS FUCKING SHIT AND SHOVE IT UP YOUR FUCKING ASS!" he yelled as he tossed everything into the briefcase. He picked it up off the table and said, "LET'S GO! YOU NEED TO FUCKING LEAVE NOW!"

With that, he went racing out the door, down the halls, briefcase in hand and me running after him. He went right to the parking lot where I was parked and as I opened up the trunk, he threw the briefcase in so violently that it popped open; some of the papers flying into the street outside and the others strewn through the trunk of the car.

He slammed the trunk closed, and screamed at me, "JUST GET THE FUCK OUT OF HERE!"

As I got into the driver's seat, I watched as he stormed back into the hospital without even a glance back at me.

CHAPTER 2

I SAT THERE IN THE parking lot for what seemed like an hour trying to compose myself. The tears were streaming down my face as I thought.

What the hell was that about? What am I going to do? How am I going to get through this? How dare he talk to me like that! Is he nuts? Am I?

There was an older woman who walked up to my car with a concerned look on her face. She'd obviously seen the whole incident with David and me. She knocked on the window to ask, "Are you okay? Is there something I can do to help you?"

I rolled down the window to speak to her. "Thanks for asking. That's very kind of you but I'll be all right. There's nothing you can do."

I wiped my eyes then, shaking myself back into reality.

I need to get home to the kids. They are my sanity. They need me. I have to be strong. Their needs must come before my own.

Somehow, I managed the drive home without incident.

I was greeted at the door by my five year old son, J.R., who looked at me with concern way beyond his years.

He said, "How's Daddy? When's he coming home?"

I sat down on the couch gathering him in my arms and hugged him tight and said, "Your dad is doing good, he just needs to stay where he is now until he feels better and the doctors tell him it's ok to come back home. Don't worry, he will be fine."

J.R. said, "I told my teacher today that Daddy was in the hospital."

"You did?" I cringed.

"Yes, I told her he was a alcohol," he said in his kindergarten way of speaking.

My eyes filled with tears then as I realized just how smart J.R. was at his tender age of five. I'm sure he'd heard conversations while I was on the phone with family members, trying to explain what was going on at our house. It shocked me just a bit that he knew but I'd always thought the best policy with the kids was to be honest. They are so accepting of the truth, no matter what.

"That's fine, Honey."

I didn't want to chastise him for giving away the family secrets. That would have confused him even more.

I hugged him again as I smiled and said, "Do you know how much I love you?"

He spread his arms open as wide as he could as he grinned from ear to ear and said, "This much?"

"That's right," I said, "Now where are your sisters?"

"They are in their room with Dolores," J.R. said.

As I walked into their bedroom with J.R. at my side, I could hear squeals of laughter as Dolores was changing Valerie's diaper.

I was so lucky to have met Dolores a few months earlier at a church group. As we got to know each other more personally, I'd shared with her what was going on in my home. It was easier to speak to her about it, a virtual stranger, rather than a family member. Turns out, she had dealt with alcoholism in her life as well, so she could relate.

That was actually my first *ah-ha* moment when I had talked to her about the craziness. It was the first time that I realized that there were many other people dealing with the same disease that I was. I'd felt so isolated before that. It was such a huge comfort knowing that she too was carrying this burden with her as well.

When David had gone into treatment, Dolores was the first person I thought of to call for help. She knew a lot of people in our church parish and I thought she might know of someone who could help me with the kids. I was so thrilled when she told me that she could actually help me out herself. I needed someone full time to take the kids where they needed to go and to cook and clean and care for them in my home, while I was at David's business for most of the day and at the hospital every evening. Dolores had a daughter named Janine who would take the shifts that Dolores could not. They were such a blessing!

There was music playing from Gina's Fischer Price record player. And as Dolores changed Valerie's diaper, both of the girls were giggling with some of their favorite music from Zoobilee Zoo. Gina was on the floor dancing like crazy to entertain her little sister and it was working like a charm.

Gina laughed and said, "Hi Mommy, come on, dance with us!"

As we entered the room, J.R. and I both joined right in and started dancing as well, which made all of us laugh even more. I laughed so hard that I cried and it was fine with me that they all thought my tears were those of joy rather than the actual panic I was feeling. My emotions at that point were totally out of control.

It felt so good to relax with the kids for just a bit. I don't know what I'd have done without them. I'd oftentimes felt like I was missing out on some special moments with the kids because my mind was so immersed in the dysfunction with David. I was constantly distracted with terrible thoughts of what was going on with him and how it was affecting all of us.

I spent a little time with the girls then and sat down on the floor to talk and laugh and tickle them. I loved my kids so fiercely. I think I would have crumbled without them. Actually there is no doubt, I would have fallen apart.

Dolores said, "Karen, I left you some dinner in the microwave. Why don't you go eat and by the time you are done, I'll have the kids all bathed and ready for bed."

"That sounds great. Thanks so much," I sighed with relief.

The moment that I walked away from the kids, my mind turned back to David.

He didn't mean to yell at me, he's going through withdrawal! Of course I'll go back to see him again tomorrow. I have to support him if there's any chance at all of him recovering fully.

Dolores had prepared a delicious roast chicken dinner with potatoes and veggies. I heated it up and when I sat down to eat I realized that I just couldn't. It wasn't physically possible. It smelled so good but as soon as I put the first bite into my mouth, I realized that I had a huge lump in my throat that wouldn't go away. The food would not go down. I was so wound up from everything going on that I couldn't eat, so I wrapped it up and put the meal into the fridge.

I looked through the mail as Dolores finished up with the kids.

Another half hour or so . . . you need to hold it together for another half hour and then the kids will be in bed and Dolores will be gone and then I can fall apart quietly.

So I put on a happy face.

"Thanks, Dolores, for all your help today," I said as I walked her to the front door. "I'll see you in the morning."

As Dolores looked into my eyes, I knew she could see the pain, and as she gave me a huge hug she said, "You are strong Karen, you will get through this. One day at a time, you can do this."

"Thanks Dolores. Thanks so much," I said as my eyes welled with tears.

As I shut the door behind her, I wiped my eyes and put on a happy face for the kids. I said, "Let's go read!"

So we all climbed into my big bed together and got comfy as I read, *THE TRUE STORY OF THE THREE LITTLE PIGS.*

As I read the book for the fourth time, because they loved it so much, they all three, started dozing comfortably next to me. I picked them up, one at a time and carried them to their beds.

As I did, I kept telling myself, *I must stay strong for them, I cannot fall apart! I will get through this for them. I will do whatever it takes to keep this family together, for them.*

And at the same time, my mind was screaming, *HOW WILL I GET THROUGH TOMORROW? HOW AM I GOING TO EXPLAIN HIS CONTINUED ABSENCE AT HIS WORK? HOW WILL I PAY THE BILLS? HOW AM I GOING TO STAY SANE?*

I dragged myself into the shower then. I let the hot water beat down on my face for a long time as I let loose with the tears, knowing the sound of the water would muffle my sobs ...

I was exhausted as I sat down on my bed to listen to my voicemails. Two of my three sisters had called to see how I was doing. My father had called as well and I could hear the concern in his voice.

I just don't have the energy to make any calls tonight, I'll do it tomorrow.

As I lay down in bed, I remembered that before David had gone into treatment, we had planned on having a New Year's Eve celebration at our house. I had invited my brothers and sisters and a few friends. All of our children were below the age of ten and I thought it would be fun to get them all together. I now wondered if I should go ahead with the plans or not.

I have five brothers and sisters and we have always been a close family, although I never felt like I could confide in them the goings on in my life associated with the alcoholism and drug addiction. It was just too embarrassing. I didn't want them to think badly of David, so I pretended that everything was okay.

Through all the turmoil in our lives, I had always tried to keep a semblance of normalcy in socializing with friends and family. Having people around me seemed to help keep me sane.

Maybe I will still have people over and maybe not. I can think about it tomorrow.

As I switched off the lamp at my bedside, I turned over, hoping to sleep and thought about everything that had led up to David being admitted to the hospital. My mind was racing.

⊰⊰⊰

About two months ago, I'd been at the library with my kids and while they were being read to by the children's librarian, I browsed through the addiction book section and found one that screamed out to me about interventions for alcoholics. I was very intrigued to say the least as I browsed the first couple of chapters. I decided to check the book out along with several books that the children had chosen.

I kept the book hidden at home, away from David's eyes. I didn't need to aggravate him anymore than he already was, all the time. I read it when he wasn't around, which was a lot of the time.

I had tried to talk to David many times about his obvious addiction to alcohol. I tried to reason with him; to tell him how different and frightening his behavior had become.

I said "You are at the bar every damn night drinking, David! You never see the kids! They are always in bed by the time you come home! Don't you see that as a problem?"

"NO! I DON'T! I JUST NEED TO BLOW OFF SOME FUCKING STEAM AND SPEND SOME FUCKING TIME WITH MY FRIENDS!" David yelled.

"You come home drunk almost every night! That's a problem!"

"DON'T BE FUCKING TELLING ME WHAT TO DO!" he shouted.

I said, "I'm just trying to tell you that I think you have a problem, you can't seem to stop yourself from drinking all the time!"

As David got up close to my face, he shouted, "YOU THINK THIS IS A PROBLEM? THIS IS NOTHING! I'LL SHOW YOU A REAL FUCKING PROBLEM IF YOU KEEP AGGRAVATING ME ABOUT THIS! I AM NOT AN ALCOHOLIC! NOW GET THE FUCK AWAY FROM ME AND LEAVE ME THE FUCK ALONE!"

As I walked away I realized that he had spit on my face with his words. I wiped it away along with my tears. He didn't notice nor did he care.

So when I read the description of what an intervention would entail, I was terrified. I almost dropped the book as my hands shook from fear. I could hear my heart pounding in my ears at the thought.

An intervention is a planned confrontation of someone with a drinking and or drug problem by their friends and loved ones. The process is meant to illustrate the damage that the person's addictions have caused the people who care. The goal is to get the person to recognize the problem and to get professional help. A small group of loved ones get together on the addict's behalf. Each participant is asked to write down what they want to say to the addicted person; a script of sorts, that describes why they believe that he needs help in overcoming his addiction and how his behavior has affected them personally.

Just the thought of confronting David in this way made my heart race! I was scared to death at the thought of it, so for that time period, I put the information in the back of my mind and put the book away, knowing that there was no way that I could ever do that. David would probably be furious! He'd probably run in the opposite direction or worse, he'd lunge at whoever got in his way and I'd be the one who would have to once again pay the price of his rage.

I most often went to bed alone. He never came home right after work. He was out at the bar. I'd go through my day of caring for the kids, giving them dinner and their baths, and putting them to bed on my own. I would make a plate of food for David and leave it in the microwave for him, for whenever he would get home. When I found that the food had been left in the microwave many times overnight uneaten, I stopped doing it.

Most nights, I'd be sleeping when David would crawl in next to me, reeking of alcohol and cigarettes.

Our sex life had become a nightmare for me. I shudder now as I think about the first time I felt like he'd raped me. He was drunk and had crawled into bed next to me.

Even though I pretended to be sleeping, he shook me awake and said, "C'mon baby, I want you now."

"I really don't want to," I whispered.

As he started touching me, he said louder, "DON'T MAKE ME FUCKING BEG!"

So rather than deal with his wrath and the possibility of his waking the kids, I went along with him, just to get it over with. He satisfied himself and then fell into a drunken sleep. After that first time, I never considered it lovemaking again because it wasn't. It was a violation.

As I woke the next morning feeling disgusted with him and with myself, I realized that the sheets next to me were wet, with his urine. He was so damn drunk, he didn't even realize that he'd wet the bed. I was horrified. And of course when I brought it up to him at another time, he completely denied it.

When I heard the back door open late on another night, I turned away from his side of the bed as he stumbled in. I didn't even dare to look in his direction. I wanted him to think that I was sleeping. All of a sudden, I felt the whole mattress that I was laying on lift off of the box spring. He let out a guttural sound like an animal growling as he tossed the whole mattress with me in it onto the floor.

I saw stars as my head hit the side of my dresser. I was shocked to say the least.

I jumped up and yelled, "WHAT THE HELL IS WRONG WITH YOU?"

David slurred his words and said, "I just neeee to sleep! Leeee me alooone!"

With that he fell onto the box spring and passed out cold.

Rather than deal with him, I just picked up my pillow and went to the living room and slept on the couch. At least I tried to.

I would dare to pick up the intervention book at every opportunity, when I was alone, to try to wrap my mind around the whole concept of confronting David at some point. I tried to force myself into realizing that this might be an answer to my prayers and that intervention was not just something that would work for other people but in fact for David and me. I tried to convince myself that I could be brave enough. I was certain by this time that David must be doing drugs as well. His behavior had become so unpredictable and erratic; I was becoming more afraid of him and just didn't know how I could continue on this path with him.

I finally began to realize that I had no choice but to confront him. I started to think that if there were other people besides myself who would tell him that they too could see that there was a problem, that he might believe it.

He'd gone to work one morning right after Christmas, and never returned home that night or even the next day. I called his work. No one had seen him. No one knew where he was. I knew there had been times when he'd been so drunk that he'd fallen asleep in his car outside whatever bar he was at so I figured that was probably the case. But when another day passed, I became quite frantic wondering where the hell he was and if he were dead or alive.

With only a little guilt, I thought about what it would be like if he were lying dead somewhere. My life would be peaceful again. My children's lives would be safe and serene again. I did in fact wish him dead sometimes. In fact, I thought that his dying would be my only way out of this mess. I never even considered divorce; it just wasn't an option in my mind. I did imagine all the different ways that he might die. He might have a heart attack during one of his fits of rage. Sometimes I would find him passed out cold in the driver's seat of his car in front of our house when I'd wake in the morning. Maybe he would have a terrible car crash and die. I thought he might get in a bar fight and end up being murdered. I thought I was stuck in this miserable situation with no way out. I was full of despair and felt like I had no one to turn to.

I'd many times thought about suicide myself as a way out of my life. I thought that maybe if I had a terrible car accident that he would be shocked into the reality of his own life and what he was doing to himself and to his family and that he would be kind and loving to me the way a husband should be. I thought if I had a terrible illness that he might finally notice me and value me as a person and not take advantage of my kindness and my love. I thought he might finally realize all the good things around him that were so valuable and good in his life. I thought those things would make him stop drinking.

My children were the only reason I held onto my sanity. If I were not here for them, who would take care of them? They needed me.

While David was gone those couple of days, I made some phone calls. I became convinced in my mind that I no longer had a choice. I had to have an intervention for David and get him into treatment. I needed to round some people up on the off chance that he would return home at some point to be a part of it.

I called my brother–in-law who had been through treatment himself and said, "Hey Denny, David has been gone for a couple of days. I don't know where he is but if he shows up soon, I need to try to get him into treatment and I need your help."

This was no surprise to him or to other friends and family. As much as I tried to hide what was going on in our lives, people around us could see that there were huge problems and that David's alcohol addiction seemed to be at the root of it all. Only the nasty details were what I could keep hidden.

He said, "I'll be happy to help you, Karen. Let me call one of the counselors at the hospital and I'll get some advice on how best to handle this whole thing, okay?"

I started to cry as I said, "Thanks so much, Denny. I appreciate whatever you can do to help us."

I called my mother-in-law next. She agreed that she could be at the intervention if it came to that, even though I could hear the doubt in her tone. The sound of her voice seemed to change though when I shared with her the fact that her son had not returned home for two days so far.

My sister-in-law knew there were big problems with her brother and was not surprised when I called her for her help as well. She agreed that she would be a part of this confrontation. No one was happy about it, but all of them agreed that it had to be done.

Three days after he'd last left our home, David called and in a panicked voice said, "I'm at a fucking hotel, I don't know how long I've been here but there are fucking people following me!"

I said, "What? Who's following you?"

He yelled, "I'M LOOKING OUT THE FUCKING WINDOW HERE AND I CAN SEE THERE ARE A FEW PEOPLE CHECKING OUT MY ROOM HERE, I DON'T KNOW WHAT THE FUCK THEY ARE GONNA DO!"

"DAVID," I shouted! "WHY WOULD SOMEONE BE FOLLOWING YOU?"

"FUCK IF I KNOW, BUT I'LL GET BACK HOME TOMORROW! I'LL BE THERE RIGHT AFTER NOON!"

And with that, he hung up the phone.

My heart was beating out of my chest as I thought about what kind of trouble he had gotten himself into.

Is he imagining the whole situation? Is he that high?

Chapter 3

A FTER I'D SPOKEN TO DAVID, it took me a few minutes to calm down enough to think about what I'd need to do to prepare for this intervention.

I checked on the kids who were playing in the other room. I changed Val's diaper, gave all three a snack and put on one of their favorite movies, *Mary Poppins.*

I asked J.R., "Please watch out for your sisters for a bit, I need to make some phone calls, okay?"

He was smart enough and intuitive enough even at his young age to hear the urgency in my voice, and like he was wise beyond his years he said with a smile on his face, "Sure Mom, I'll babysit for you."

Gina said, "Watch with us, Mommy!"

"Just give me a few minutes," I said. "I have to make a few phone calls and I'll be right with you, okay?"

"Okay," she said with her adorable little smile. With that she found her spot on the floor next to her brother and sister and settled into the movie and snacks.

I went to my bedroom and shut the door and dialed my brother-in-law's number first.

When he answered I said, "Hi Denny . . . David called. He says that he will be home tomorrow. I hope he means it. I hope he will show up. Can you be here to help me try to get him into treatment?"

"Karen, I spoke to a counselor from the hospital," said Denny. "His name is Steve. He told me that he would not be available this weekend to be present at your house but he could be a few days later. We really should have a professional there to help us."

I said desperately, "We can't wait. We have to do this tomorrow if he shows up! Please, you've been through this. I need your help Denny. I'm afraid of him. He can't be here with me and the kids anymore . . . not the way that he's behaving. I can't feel safe this way. He has to get help!"

Denny said, "Okay, I'll definitely be there. I can't say for sure what will happen but I'll do the best I can to help."

"Thank you so much. That means so much to me. Can you be here right before noon tomorrow?"

"I'll be there. I'll call Steve back and tell him that we are going to give this thing a try. I'll ask him if there is an available bed at the hospital so that we can take him there if he agrees."

"Okay Denny, I'll see you tomorrow," I said. "I need to call a few more people who have promised to help as well, and I need to make arrangements for the kids."

"All right Karen, I love ya. I'll do my best! I'll see you tomorrow before noon. If anything changes just let me know and I'll do the same."

I called back one of David's best friends, my mother-in-law, and my sister-in-law, and they all agreed to be at my house the following day.

I called my dad then. I had tried to keep most of my angst from him but he'd sensed for a while that things were not right with David and me.

I said, "Dad, I need a favor from you. Things have not been going very well here with David and me. David's drinking has pretty much gotten totally out of control. I'm going to try to get him to go into treatment to make him stop."

He said, "Karen, I've known there's been a problem for a long time. I'm not blind. I've noticed how much he drinks and how belligerent he gets with you and the kids sometimes. You don't know how many times I've wanted to pull him aside and give him a piece of my mind!"

Here I'd thought that I'd hidden it so well. It was like the floodgates opened, talking to my dad openly about the chaos that had become my life.

Through my tears I said, "I'm sorry that I haven't talked to you about this sooner but I just couldn't. It's too hard to talk about and I kept hoping it would get better but it's only gotten worse."

My dad said, "Oh please don't worry about me, I'm worried for you. What can I do to help?"

"David's been gone for a couple of days. I'm sure he's been drinking a lot and I don't know what else he's been doing but he called today and said he would be home tomorrow afternoon. I hope that he will show up because I have a plan that I hope will work to get him into the hospital to get sober."

My dad asked, "Okay, what's the plan?"

"Denny is coming over with a few other people who are close to David and we are all going to try to convince him that he needs help to overcome his addictions. I don't know how he will react to this confrontation. In fact, I'm afraid he could become violent and I need the kids to be out of the house. Can you please come by tomorrow morning and pick them up and take them to your house for most of the day?"

"Of course I can. What time do you want me to be there?"

"How about ten o'clock?"

"That would be fine, yes," he said.

"J.R. knows there is something up. The girls are really too little to realize. I'm just going to tell them that you are picking them up for a fun visit so don't tell them anything else, okay? I'll explain more to J.R. when I can."

My dad replied, "Of course Karen, whatever you want. You know how much I love you and I am here to support you in whatever you need."

"I love you too, Dad. Thanks. I think I'll even pack them an overnight bag in case they need to stay with you if that's all right with you."

I could hear him choking up as he said, "That's fine Karen, no problem. Now go take care of those kids and I'll see you in the morning. I love you."

I could hardly get the words out with the huge lump that was in my throat but I said, "I'll see you then, Dad. I love you too."

I hung up the phone then and realized that this would probably take place now as long as David showed up. I was beyond nervous. I was terrified!

I took a few minutes to wipe my eyes and to stop my heart from racing and went to check on the kids. Valerie had actually fallen asleep as she watched the movie with her older sister and brother, right in J.R.'s lap. He smiled at me as I whispered, "I love you, thanks for being such a good brother."

As I cozied up on the couch with Gina, and as I watched the movie with them, I tried to lose myself on the chimney tops with the sweepers who were dancing and jumping from rooftop to rooftop.

I was so emotionally exhausted that J.R. was the one to shake me awake when the movie was over, "Mom, get up, the movie's over."

"Okay," I said with a smile.

"Look out the front window!" J.R. yelled. "It's snowing really hard!"

All of us looked out the window to see that the new accumulation now gave us enough snow to go out and play. The flakes were huge.

I said, "Well, what are you all waiting for? Get your snow suits on! Get your mittens and hats and boots! Let's go out and play!"

They all squealed with delight as I thanked God up above for these miracles who were my children. They had become my everything. They were all that mattered to me. I had to create a safe and loving home for them. They were my reason for getting up in the morning. They were my hope that David would recover from this addiction that had become his life, so that he could be a father to them and play that ever important role in our children's lives.

They went running to their rooms as J.R. yelled, "First thing I'm gonna do is make a whole pile of snowballs, Mom! You think they will last out there till Daddy gets home?"

"I'm not sure but we can certainly try," I said.

So as it goes with little ones . . . about twenty minutes later after finding all their snow gear, we were out in our little yard having the time of our lives. As promised, J.R. went to work gathering up the snow in his little hands, creating snowballs. I lay down in the snow to show my girls how to make snow angels. And when J.R. started throwing snowballs in our direction, Gina and Val and I laughed as we hid behind the flying saucers that I'd bought for them the previous week after we'd gotten the first substantial snowfall.

When Valerie's little fingers looked frozen and when J.R. finally got tired of throwing snowballs, I was able to convince them to come inside, when I tempted them with hot chocolate with the miniature marshmallows they loved. So we all piled into the back door and down the stairs where we hung all the clothes to dry and headed back upstairs for the promised drink.

As they drank, I prepared them some dinner and as we ate, it became dark outside which made the falling snow even prettier.

I said, "Look out the window now . . . look how pretty the snow looks! See how it glitters on the ground?"

"I wish Daddy could see it," Gina said with a pensive look on her face. "When is Daddy going to be home?"

"He should be home tomorrow, Honey. He called earlier, he's okay," I lied.

"Let's get your bath ready, girls. You will go after them, J.R. I have a surprise for all of you!"

"What's the surprise?" J.R. asked with excitement.

"Grandpa B is picking you all up in the morning. He called today and said that he missed you all so much that he wants to have some special time with all of you! I'm even going to pack you what you need for overnight. I'm sure that Grandpa has fun plans for you!"

Gina and Val held hands and jumped up and down laughing.

J.R. said, "You think Grandpa knows how to make snowballs?"

"Uh . . . yeah!" I laughed and said, "Who do you think taught me?"

"GRANDPA!" J.R. shouted.

"That's right," I said.

After they had all been bathed, we sat down to read and one by one like usual, I carried them each to their own beds and said good night.

As soon as the last was in bed, my thoughts went right back to David. I was hoping that he was safe and at the same time wishing he would never come back.

I took a shower and got comfortable sitting up in bed and picked up the intervention book and began to read the parts that I hadn't yet and the parts again that I had, and tried to prepare myself for what lay ahead of me tomorrow.

I read that people had once believed that an alcoholic had to reach their bottom on their own in order to get help. Their bottom was defined as the time in their life where they could finally see for themselves that their addictions were creating so much heartache and chaos and ruin, that they would seek help for themselves. But it was later realized that we can create their bottom.

How great is that? Maybe I can make this happen!

Intervention is a way of raising their bottom. An intervention can be an organized and loving act performed by friends and family. We no longer have to stand on the sidelines just waiting for that freight train of disaster to hit. We can create a bottom of sorts that will help to persuade them into getting help. It's sometimes referred to as a shakeup intervention.

As I read further, the book talked about the most common enemy of a successful intervention to be denial. That was what I feared most; denial and rage directed at me for daring to talk to other people about what David thought had been kept under wraps. I thought he would surely be furious at me. I had tried to reassure myself though, that having other people around would at least keep me from physical harm, for the moment anyway.

But I knew that I no longer had a choice. I had to do this. The situation had become too dangerous for me and the kids. Something had to change.

My ultimate goal was to get David to go into a thirty day treatment center, the way that Denny had. He had gone through the program a couple of years previously and seemed to be getting his life back together in a productive way. Honestly though, I felt that the chances were very slim that David would agree. He had been in such denial for so long; I didn't really think that he would see what a disaster his life had become.

I dozed off as I read but did wake with a start several times during the night. My mind was racing and my heart was pounding with thoughts of the next day.

Will he show up? How mad is he going to be? Will there be a physical fight between David and Denny? What the hell am I going to do if he doesn't agree to get help?

I was wide awake early that next morning. There was no resting now. I picked up the book that was still lying next to me and put it in my dresser drawer underneath some clothes.

I took a deep breath and whispered out loud, "Dear God, please let him show up today. Please help me to have the courage to do this. Please let him agree to get help."

I heard Valerie crying in her crib then, and I jumped up to take care of her.

"What's wrong pumpkin . . . did you have a bad dream?" I asked as I hugged her and stroked her hair. She loved when I played with her hair; it always seemed to soothe her.

"Okay, let's get breakfast for you, and J.R., and Gina! You have a fun day coming up with Grandpa and we need to get you ready," I said.

As we ate breakfast we noticed all the snow that had fallen.

"Look J.R.," I said. "All those snowballs that you left out last night are covered with new snow!"

"Oh no!" J.R. said. "I wanted to play with those snow balls with Daddy."

I said, "Don't worry. The snow on top of them will be like a refrigerator . . . they will be there when you want them. And we can always make fresh ones if we need to."

I got the kids all dressed and fed and packed their overnight bags. They watched cartoons while they waited for their grandpa to pick them up.

The snow was still falling and I hoped that the roads would not be too slick for everyone to arrive at my house as planned.

The doorbell rang and the kids all jumped up.

"GRANDPA!" they all shouted in unison.

My dad had a big smile on his face as I opened the door and he could see all three kids laughing and excited.

I said "Grab your coats and hats and mittens, hurry up! Grandpa is anxious to go!"

As the kids ran to their rooms my dad said, "I'll keep the kids for as long as you need, Karen. David had better go into treatment! I don't trust him here with you and the kids anymore!"

"I know Dad, I can't trust him anymore either. His temper has been so unpredictable and violent! He's out of control."

"If he dares to threaten you, I swear I'm going to let him have it, damnit!"

"I know Dad. If he doesn't agree to go, somehow I'll have to make him leave. It's just not safe for him to be here."

"Please . . . call me later and let me know how it goes," he said.

I said, "Of course I will. Wish us luck! We are going to need it for sure!!"

My dad said, "You know I only wish the best for you. God bless you Karen."

And with that the kids were running back to us screaming with delight.

"LET'S GO GRANDPA!"

I knelt down on the floor to help the girls with their coats and hats and boots and handed each of them their backpacks and said, "You are going to have so much fun! I will miss you!"

At that both the girls wrapped their arms around me at the same time and hugged me so tight that I almost fell on the floor.

We all laughed as Gina said, "I love you, Mommy! I hope you have fun, too."

"Oh, I'll be just fine," I said.

J.R. hugged me the tightest and when he looked at me with that knowing look in his eyes he said, "I'll help you with all the shoveling when I get back, Mom."

"You better," I said with a smile.

Valerie said, "Bye bye, Mommy."

And as they all rambled out the door into the snow I said, "Sorry Dad, that I didn't get to shovel the walk yet, I'm going to do that now. The fresh cold air will do me good."

"Okay, I'll talk to you soon, Karen, love you."

"Thanks, Dad, love you too. Bye bye, have fun!" I said to all of them.

As I closed and locked the door behind them and watched my dad's car pull away, I felt good knowing that they would not be subjected to whatever might happen here at the house with this day's events.

They had already been witness to too much insanity. As much as I tried to shelter them from David's ugly words and volatile temper, they heard him yelling at me. They saw him having fits of rage, throwing things around the house. They knew that something was wrong. The girls were just too young to express it.

And J.R. on many occasions would cower in fear from his father and ask me later, "Why is Daddy being so mean?"

I'd try to cover for him and say, "He doesn't mean it . . . he's just had a bad day."

That was when the lying began and the covering up for David became a habit. I was always making excuses for him. I suppose lying about his behavior helped me to get through each day and helped to ease my mind as well as the kids.

There was no question about where David worked, once you caught a whiff of him as he walked in the door at the end of the day. The smell, which was a mix of gasoline and car exhaust, was unmistakable. He usually had stains on his uniform shirt and his hair was greasy. That's just the way it is in that profession.

I tried to ignore it the first time that it happened but after I'd noticed it several times, I had to ask. As he came in, he gave me a peck on the cheek. I couldn't help but notice.

I said, "Hmmm, you must not have worked very hard today. You smell so clean."

David asked, "What are you talking about?"

I said, "This isn't the first time that I've noticed David. Do you really think I'm an idiot?"

He said with an innocent look on his face, "I don't know what you mean."

I said, "I've noticed several times lately that you come home from work and you smell like you've taken a shower. What's up with that?"

"You're fuckin crazy," said David.

"No! I'm not! You can't deny it! There is no shower at your work! Where are you showering?"

"I don't know what you're talking about," he said a bit nervously.

I shouted, "DON'T TREAT ME LIKE A FOOL! WHERE THE HELL ARE YOU CLEANING UP AFTER WORK?"

He shouted back, "IT'S NO BIG DEAL. I'M GOING TO A FRIEND'S HOUSE TO RELAX FOR A WHILE! I USE THEIR SHOWER!"

"WHO IS IT?"

"IT'S JUST A FRIEND!"

I screamed, "WHO IS SHE?"

David said quietly then, "Who said it was a she?"

I was dumbfounded as he walked away. Speechless . . .

Huh?

There was never any other explanation.

I never talked to anyone about it. How could I? It was too embarrassing, wasn't it? What was I supposed to think?

And I chose to never question it again. Stuffed it down. Pushed it out of my mind, out of my thoughts . . . like so many things . . .

—◈—◈—◈—

Today, I put on my coat and gloves and went outside on the porch to retrieve the shovel that was leaning up against the wall there, and went to work on the front walk so there would be a clear path from the street to the house. The snow was quite deep and heavy and was still coming down pretty hard and steady. I felt like my face was being pelted with ice shards, the wind was blowing so badly. It was almost cleansing in a way.

My next door neighbor waved and said hi as I shoveled and cried. I don't think he noticed my tears; my face was wet with snow as well. As I waved back, I prayed.

Dear God, give me courage to do this. Don't let me crumble. I have to do this for the kids. Help me God.

I was terrified at what lay ahead in just a couple of hours.

Then when I couldn't lift another shovel full, I went into the house and took off all my wet clothing and got into a nice hot shower and just let the water beat on my face. I washed away the tears and just resolved myself to the fact that this confrontation would happen today as long as David showed up. I got out of the shower and put on a sweatshirt and jeans. After I dried my hair, I put on just a touch of makeup knowing full well that today might very well be just another day of many, where I'd cry it off anyway.

As I finished in the bathroom, the doorbell rang. It was Denny.

"Hi Denny," I said with a huge sigh. "Are you ready for this?"

"Ready as I'll ever be, Karen," he said with a smile.

"Have you heard from David today?" Den asked.

"No, but he said yesterday that he would be here after noon. It's getting close to that now so hopefully, he will be here."

Denny said, "I talked to that counselor Steve, and he gave me a few tips to share with everyone who will be here."

"Great," I said, "They should all be here soon and we can talk about it, okay?"

"Yes, that would be good. I hope we can do this. I hope we can convince him to get help."

"So do I. I'm really scared, Denny," I said.

He gave me a hug then and said, "It will be all right, Karen, no matter what."

"Keep telling me that, maybe it will help me get through this day."

Denny said, "The best news is that there is a bed available at the hospital for David to go through detox if he agrees to go. Steve gave me the direct number to call if we are heading there later to admit him."

"I'm not sure how he's going to react, Denny, so be prepared. I hope that it doesn't get physical," I said.

Denny laughed as he said, "I hope not too, but I can take care of myself, no worries!"

The doorbell rang again and as I looked out the window on the door, I saw that it was my expected guests. I opened the door to my mother-in-law, Rita, my sister- in-law, Kim, and a longtime friend of both David and I, Brad.

I gave them each a hug as they walked in and I said, "Thanks so much for being here. I know this is not a pleasant thing to do but I can't do it without all of you."

Brad gave me another big hug and said, "I'm so sorry it's come to this, Karen. I've seen such a change in David lately in such a bad way. I hope I can help."

"Just being here is helpful, Brad. I really appreciate it."

Kim said, "I'll do whatever I can to help, Karen. I'm sorry things have been so shitty for you."

"Thanks Kim," I said as my eyes welled with tears. "Come in everybody. Let's go to the kitchen and get some coffee, okay? Hopefully David will be here soon."

As we walked to the kitchen, Rita said, "Do you really think this is necessary, Karen? Are things really that bad?"

"Yes Rita," I said with a huge sigh, "it's been my mistake not talking about what's been going on here sooner, things have gotten totally out of control."

I could tell she still doubted my words, and I was beginning to wonder if Rita was a good choice at all to have here. David was her little boy and she felt that he could do no wrong.

Oh well, nothing I can do about that now. We just have to roll with this.

So after we all got something to drink, I ushered them all back into the living room to wait for David.

As we all found our seats, Denny said, "This is what we all need to think about. Up until now, David has thought that his current behavior has not been detected by any of us. He thinks that Karen is nuts and that she's making things up to make him look bad. He thinks there is no problem."

"That's exactly the case," I said.

Denny said, "What we need to do here is to tell David in our own words what we have seen change in him. We need to tell him that his behavior and his drinking have affected all of us in a negative way."

Brad said, "Even his appearance has changed dramatically over the last few months. I hardly recognize him. He's gained so much weight. It's like he doesn't even care anymore."

Denny said, "That's what alcohol and drug addiction do to you. We need to tell him that we care about him and that he needs to do himself a favor and get professional help."

"I've noticed in the way he treats the kids," said Kim, "that there is definitely something wrong."

Even Rita admitted then, "I've seen it when we all go out for dinner. He can down ten rum and cokes in the time it takes to have dinner served to us."

"You probably didn't know this Rita but it's been on those occasions that I've been terrified to have him drive me and the kids home and he insists on driving. He's passed out in front of the house as soon as we get here. But he'll admit to nothing the next day and just claim that he was tired," I said.

"So let's all give this a bit of thought," Denny said. "Think about what you want to say to him when he gets here and maybe let's all say a prayer that he gets the help that he needs to get better. If I can do it, anyone can."

I sat in the recliner right by the front window for what seemed like hours waiting for him to arrive as he'd promised. The others in the room were talking to each other. I didn't really hear a word of what they were saying. As I looked around the room, I saw their lips moving but heard nothing. I was lost inside my head. I was a nervous wreck.

At about twelve fifteen, my heart just about beat out of my chest when I saw him pull up to the front of the house.

Oh my God, he's here.

I said out loud, "He's here, Denny."

Denny said, "Okay everyone, we can do this, take a deep breath and get ready."

I was frozen in the chair where I sat. I couldn't get up. I couldn't move. I was paralyzed with fear.

David used his key to get into the front door.

As he walked in, he looked so disheveled and dirty. He just reeked of cigarette smoke. His eyes were puffy like he hadn't slept. He didn't even have a coat on. He had on the same clothes he had on a couple of days ago when he left. He looked around the room to see all of us.

And as he glared at me he said angrily "What the fuck are you all doing here?"

CHAPTER 4

DENNY WAS UP ON HIS feet right away and as he shook David's hand he looked him square in the eye and said, "David . . . we are all here for you. We want to talk to you."

And as David looked in my direction he said through clenched teeth, "What the fuck have you been telling them?"

"I didn't really have to tell them anything, David. Anyone can see that you are not yourself. We want you to get help," I said softly.

As David moved fast towards me he spit in my face as he yelled, "THERE'S NOTHING WRONG WITH ME, WHAT THE FUCK ARE YOU TALKING ABOUT? HELP FOR WHAT?"

"Whoa! Whoa David! Calm down! Give me a chance to explain what we're doing here," said Denny as he got between us. "This right here, right now, this is the problem! Why would you talk to your wife like that? It's not right. It's not like you."

David backed away from me a bit. He seemed to hear what Denny had said. He had always liked Denny. He had considered him one of his best friends. Denny seemed to have a calming effect on David.

"C'mon David, have a seat. Let's talk," said Denny.

"Fine!" said David as he sat on the recliner at the other end of the room.

Denny said, "Karen, why don't you get David a cup of coffee while he catches his breath and we can explain to him why we are here . . . okay?"

"Sure," I said as I shook myself out of my head into the reality of what was happening.

I could feel David glaring at me as I walked out of the room.

I could hear Denny say, "Take a deep breath, David . . . calm down and get ready to listen to us. Please."

When I came back into the living room with coffee, Denny began to explain.

"David, we are all here because we care about you. Karen cares the most. That's why she called me and confided in me her concerns for you. We all think that your drinking and your drug use has become an overwhelming obstacle for you. You are not yourself. We want to help you."

"I don't need any help, Denny," said David very calmly. "I'm fine."

Denny said, "Please just listen to what we have to say and then you can choose how to handle this whole thing, okay?"

"Okay," said David.

As David looked at Denny, I noticed just how bloated his face looked. He had dark circles under his eyes. He hadn't shaved in several days. His hair was dirty and I saw that his hands were shaking. I couldn't help but notice all the weight he had gained as well over the last several months. His appearance was shocking.

Denny said, "David, I know what you are going through. I know better than most people. I am you . . . you know I've been there just like you. So please just hear us out, all right?"

"Fine . . . okay," David said with a sigh.

Denny said, "Brad, can you start us off here and tell David what's on your mind?"

"Yes," said Brad. "I've been one of your best friends for a long time, David, and I am afraid for you. I've so admired over the years the way that you have taken care of yourself. You and I used to play racquetball all the time. You could kick my ass on that court! You took such pride in how you looked. You were lifting weights and keeping yourself in really good shape. And now as I look at you, I can see you are not healthy. I hardly recognize you."

As I observed this conversation going on, I could hardly believe that David actually seemed to be listening! He wasn't yelling at anyone! My biggest fears for today did not seem to be coming to fruition.

This is going much better than I thought it would . . . Thank you God!

Brad went on to say, "You seem to be totally distracted by something else going on in your life and it's obviously not something good. You are ignoring the things in your life that are the most important. Your drinking is what seems to be out of control. It's not like you to ignore your health the way that you seem to be lately. And when I talk to Karen, I can hear the fear in her voice and she knows you better than any of us do. I know how much you have always loved Karen, and I know you don't mean to hurt her in any way. I'm here today to ask you to take better care of yourself. Karen and the kids need you. I need my friend to be healthy. I'm asking you to get the help that we are suggesting to you today."

David said, "Okay . . . I hear you."

David was pretending to be calm with what was going on around him, even though I knew that he was probably fuming inside. He was such a good actor. He could convince those around him that he was just fine and except for his outburst when he arrived he was able to control himself and his emotions but I feared what might happen when everybody left us alone.

There's no way he can stay here at the end of this day. I won't be safe. Even if he doesn't go to the hospital for the help that he needs, he can't stay here.

Denny said, "Do you mind going next Kim?"

I could see David glancing at me with what seemed like a pleading look in his eye. His look said why are you doing this to me? I tried not to look in his direction. I kept my head down and listened to what everyone was saying.

Kim said, "I don't mind, no." She looked at David and teared up as she said, "I'm here because I love you, big brother, and I'm concerned for you. Karen has confided in me, about what's been going on with you. You are absent here and you seem to be at the bars all the time instead of here with Karen and the kids."

David said, "I'm at fuckin work all the time!"

Kim said, "Where are you after work?"

"Well yeah, I like to go to the bar after work with my buddies," David said. "But I don't have a problem."

"But you have this great family at home waiting for you. You have three beautiful kids at home here who need you. I'm here to visit pretty often and when I'm here with them, I'm very often wondering where you are because you are not at work twenty four hours a day. You are missing out on so much. They are such good kids."

"I know that," David said quietly.

Kim went on, "The only reason that I can come up with as to why you would go to the bar then, instead of coming home is that you can't stop yourself. I believe you have a problem and I'm asking you today to get the help that you deserve."

Denny said, "Thanks Kim. Can you tell David what's on your mind now, Rita?"

Rita said, "Yes I can. We all care about you here, David, and as your mother, I just want you to be happy. I met up with you at the bar a couple of weeks ago and we had a long talk and I thought that you were okay but Karen seems to think differently."

"I really am okay, Mom. You don't have to worry," said David.

Rita said, "I do know this. I've noticed that the last couple of times we've gone out to dinner as a family, that you can down rum and cokes like there's no tomorrow. I don't know where you're putting it, but with the amount that you're drinking I'm surprised you are not passed out under the table."

David smiled as he said, "Aww c'mon, Mom, it's not that bad. They're really small glasses!"

"I don't think it's funny, David, and I am concerned for you and Karen and the kids. If you feel like you need some help here, just say so."

"All right Mom, I hear you," said David.

Denny said, "Can you go next, Karen?"

"Yes," I said as I took a deep breath and sighed. "David . . . have you looked at yourself in the mirror lately? Because when I look at you, I'm terrified. You scare me. You scare the kids. Your behavior is totally out of control. I don't know you anymore."

And as I started to cry, he looked at me like he actually cared. I hadn't seen a kind look on his face for many months. I was convinced that he hated me, but right now I was actually seeing just a glimmer of the David who cared about me and my feelings . . . just a glimmer.

"I'm really okay, Karen," said David.

"No, you're not," I said. "I'm asking you today to please get some help. What you are doing is not working. Something has to change. I can't continue to allow this behavior around the kids."

David said, "What is it you expect me to do?"

"Denny called the hospital where he was in treatment. There's an open bed there right now. You can be admitted to their program today."

He said, "WHAT ARE YOU FUCKING CRAZY? I CAN'T DO THAT! I HAVE A FUCKING BUSINESS TO RUN!"

Denny chimed right in then and said, "If you don't take care of yourself David, there will be no business left. Seems to me that things are not going too well there lately, am I right?"

David said, "Business has been kind of slow lately, that's true. But that's to be expected with the transition from being in a partnership to being just a single owner now."

Denny asked, "Why did that happen, David? What happened to your partner?"

"He was messing everything up! He's a fucking asshole! I don't need him. I bought him out," David replied.

Denny said, "Okay . . . what if I promised to spend some time at your business helping you out to keep it running while you take care of yourself? Then will you take me up on this offer to get you into a program that can help you to think more clearly again?"

David said, "How long of a program?"

Denny said, "It's a thirty day program."

"Oh my God, are you fucking kidding me? There's just no fucking way I can do that. I don't have that luxury of time!"

Brad spoke up then and said, "I'll help you out too David. I can spend some time at your service station and do what needs to be done."

I was sure as Brad said these words that he really didn't know what this kind of responsibility would mean but at this point I really didn't care.

WHATEVER IT TAKES! SAY WHATEVER YOU HAVE TO SAY TO CONVINCE HIM TO GO!

As David shook his head, he said "No, it's just not possible, I have a family to support and I do that through my business. I can't be away for thirty fucking days."

David glared at me like a caged lion as he spoke. The arguments went back and forth for over an hour between Denny and Kim and Brad until Denny spoke up louder.

Denny said, "Karen, what's going to happen today if David decides not to go into treatment?"

I looked at David and said with new found bravery, "You will have to find somewhere else to stay, because in the condition you're in, you can't stay here. I love you but I can't trust you. I'm afraid of you and you cannot be around the kids unless you make an effort to get help."

David said, "Are you fucking kidding me?"

I answered, "No, I'm not. You leave me no choice. I'm begging you . . . please get help."

Denny said, "We've all seen changes in you, David. Disturbing and frightening changes. We are asking you to get help. You have to take care of yourself first or everything else in your life is going to crumble down around you. If you can't be one hundred percent focused on your business, there will be no business left for you anyway. I'm asking you as well. Please get help. Let me take you to the hospital right now."

There were a couple of long minutes of silence then. David looked around the room at each one of us, and when his eyes ended up on me he said, "Fine, I'll go for you, Karen."

Oh my God! He's going into treatment! Yippee! I can't believe this worked!

I said, "Really?"

"Yes, I'll go for you, Karen."

Denny said, "Okay, let me make a phone call and tell them that we are on our way, David."

As Denny walked out of the room to make the call, Kim walked up to David and as she hugged him she said, "You're making the right choice bro, I love you."

"Yeah, I'll get this over with, I'll go for Karen," David said.

Rita gave David a quick hug and said, "It's time for us to get going Kim, let's get out of their way here."

David looked a little shell shocked as Brad shook his hand and told him, "We're all here for you, Buddy. I'll help Karen with whatever she needs. Take care of yourself."

And with that, Brad, Kim, and Rita were out the front door.

Denny had warned me beforehand that if David agreed to go into treatment, it was something we needed to do in a hurry, before he had a chance to change his mind.

Denny hung up the phone and said, "They are awaiting our arrival. Karen, let me take David to the hospital. You take care of the kids and whatever else you need to take care of here. I've got this covered. It's getting late and all they will do today is to get him admitted and into a room. You can come and see him tomorrow."

It was all happening so quickly now but I trusted Denny to do the right thing.

I said, "Do we need to pack him a suitcase, Denny?"

"No, they will supply whatever he needs for tonight. You can bring a few of his things tomorrow."

I said, "Okay."

Denny said, "Let's go, David. They are waiting for us."

David said, "I'll do this for you Karen, I'm going for you."

I don't care why you're going, just go! Hurry up before you have any more time to think about it! GO!

As I hugged him goodbye I said, "I'll see you tomorrow. I love you."

David said in kind of a daze, "Okay, I'll see you then. I love you to . . . I'm doing this for you."

He walked out the front door and I gave Denny a quick hug as he walked behind him. I mouthed the words to Denny, *thank you.*

As I watched them drive away, I realized that I'd never felt so all alone in my life.

Chapter 5

It was the day before New Year's Eve when my sister called to see how the kids and I were doing.

Nancy said, "How's everything going, Karen?"

I said, "David's gotten through the worst part of detox I guess. I'll see him tonight after I go to the gas station and try to figure some things out there. I have just a couple of minutes before Dolores gets here."

She said, "But how are you doing, Karen? Are you okay?"

"I'm feeling pretty shaky but I'm getting better. At least I'm not afraid to be in my own house wondering if and when David will show up and what condition he will be in! And I figure he's safe where he is for now."

Nancy said, "How's everything going at his work?"

"I was there all day yesterday. It's such a joke! I had to meet with one of his bosses from the oil company and I had to lie about where David is. I'm a terrible liar. I don't know if he believed me or not," I said.

"Karen, I'm so sorry that things are so crazy for you right now. I'm here for you, whenever you need to talk."

"I appreciate that."

Nancy said, "I know you were going to have a party for New Year's Eve. I'm sure you have decided to cancel, yes?"

"Actually, I was thinking I would go ahead and have you all over anyway."

Nancy said, "Seriously?"

I said, "I figured I have a choice. I can stay home alone with the kids and cry and be miserable thinking about everything or I can try to get my mind off of it even if it's just for a moment. Having all of you around me will help. The kids will love having all of you here and I just want to do the best that I can for them. I think that it will help us all get through this."

Nancy said, "If you are sure. We can all bring appetizers and drinks and we'll all just be together."

I said, "I think that will work, yes. I'm not going to the gas station tomorrow. Thank God David seems to have one employee that I think I can trust to help me figure some things out there because in the state of mind that David's in now, I can't get any help from him. I have no choice really . . . I have to trust Tom. He said that he will take care of things tomorrow for me, and New Year's Day they will be closed, so that gives me two days off."

"Tell me what time you want us over and I'll let everyone else know," Nancy said.

"Let's make it about seven thirty, okay? I don't plan on going to the hospital tomorrow. They are not doing too much as far as therapy goes on New Year's Eve or the day after. I've been told that it's going to get really serious after that because his mind and body should be pretty cleared from the alcohol and whatever else he was doing."

Nancy said, "What else do you think he was doing?"

I said, "I think that he's been using cocaine. On more than one occasion when he's come home, I've noticed a white powder on his nose. When I asked him about it, he just wiped it away and said it was nothing."

"Oh my God! Are you kidding me?" she asked.

"No, I never said anything because I didn't want to believe it myself so I let it go."

"Oh Karen, I feel so bad for you," Nancy said.

"I know," I said. "But I have to go now. I'll see you tomorrow night and we can talk more then."

"That sounds great," said Nancy. "I'll see you tomorrow."

As soon as I hung up the phone, the doorbell rang.

"Mommy, it's Dolores," yelled J.R. "Do you want me to let her in?"

"No!" I replied. "You remember my rule, don't you?"

J.R. laughed and said, "I do but tell me again!"

As I walked to the front door, I said, "You are NEVER to open the door to anyone when I'm not right there with you; ESPECIALLY if I'm not home. You NEVER open the door! And remember, even if Jesus Christ were at the door, he would want you to listen to your mom and not open that door without me!"

I could hardly get those words out without laughing but it was one of my biggest rules to keep us all safe.

J.R. said, "Okay Mommy!"

This Chicago winter was getting colder and I shuddered a bit as the wind whipped inside the house when I opened the door.

"Hi Dolores, how are you today?"

As she hugged me she said, "I'm just fine, Karen, what about you?"

"I'm doing all right," I said.

I'd already given the kids their breakfast and they were watching a movie, still in their pajamas, as I got ready to go.

As Dolores cleaned up the kitchen she said, "I'll get them dressed. Don't you worry about a thing, Karen. You go take care of what you need to."

The kids already adored Dolores and her daughter Janine, thank God. I don't know what I'd have done without them.

"Thanks Dolores, c'mon kids, give me hugs. I'll see you later around dinnertime."

Gina said, "Why do you have to go, Mommy? Watch the movie with us please?"

"I'm sorry, I can't today, Sweetie. I have to take care of some things for Daddy. You be a good girl and listen to Dolores, okay?"

"Okay," she said with a frown. "Where is Daddy? When's he coming home?"

"He has to spend a little more time in the hospital. He's not feeling very good and the doctors are going to fix him up as good as new," I said with a smile. I tried to distract her then by saying, "We are going to have a party tomorrow though! Your cousins will all be here. We will have lots of fun together, okay?"

"YIPPEE!" all three of them yelled with excitement.

"So please be good for Dolores today, and I'll see you later."

"Okay Mommy," said Gina.

I gave them all a big hug and I was out the door into the cold day.

As I got into the car, I thought ahead of what I hoped to accomplish at the gas station today. I was really leaning on Tom to help guide me in the routine of the business. I had to write payroll checks. Each employee was making a different wage and Tom had promised to help me figure all that out. I had to make bank deposits; one for payroll and one for purchasing auto parts and gasoline. I counted on Tom to help me order whatever supplies we needed as well.

My mind was racing, always racing.

What's David doing now? Is he going to be okay through all this? Will we be able to save this troubled marriage? How can I ever trust him again?

I'd first met David when I was only thirteen years old, just a baby really. The first time I'd laid eyes on him was when I was at the grocery store one day with my mother. He was stocking shelves as we walked by. I saw him looking at me. I looked back at him as well.

The next week, when my mom asked me to help her with the shopping again, I made a point of checking myself out in the mirror beforehand to brush my hair and to put on a bit of lip gloss. I was thinking in the back of my mind.

Maybe he will be there again.

I remembered how my heart pounded just a bit that first time when I'd caught him looking at me.

This time he made a point of coming out to the parking lot as my mom and I left with a cart full of groceries. I could see him gathering up carts in the parking lot and as I walked our empty cart back to the designated area, he was there and said to me, "Can I put that back for you?"

"Sure," I said.

"Take care," he said with a smile.

"Thanks," I said, very timidly.

It was funny the next time I saw him was at my high school. I attended an all girls' high school and right across the schools' parking lot was an all boys' high school. We were allowed outside after eating our lunch for some fresh air and the boys would flirt with the girls and the girls would flirt with the boys from across the lot. This day, one of the girls noticed that there were several boys passing around a pair of binoculars trying to get a better look. It was all in good fun and a bunch of us were laughing as I noticed that one of the boys was David.

When I attended the first school dance of the year over at the boys' school is when I met David again. I loved going to the dances. I'd attended a couple of them while I was still in junior high and found that it was a great place to make new friends and have fun. I loved to dance . . . it was such a great way to blow off steam. There was at least one high school in our area each weekend that would sponsor a dance. There were live bands that played, and lots of kids from all over the area would meet.

I'd arrived at this dance with my sister. My mom probably would not have let me attend without her guidance. I was happy to be there but still rather shy at my age.

David walked up to me and said, "Want to dance?"

My sister looked at him and then at me and said, "Go ahead, Karen."

So I said with a smile to David, "You're that guy from the grocery store, aren't you?"

David said with a smile, "I am. C'mon, you want to dance?"

"Okay, sure."

It was a fast dance and there were lots of kids on the dance floor and the music was great so it was really fun.

He was immediately possessive. He asked me to dance just about every dance but I really wanted to meet other people that night as well so I did turn him down a couple of times. He asked my sister to dance then and eyed me as he did, wanting some kind of reaction from me, I suppose.

We ended up dancing several times and there were a couple of slow dances where he held me tight. I have to admit I liked it. It felt good, and right before the lights were turned up signifying that it was time for the evening to end, he asked me, "Can I have your phone number? I'd like to call you if that's okay."

"Okay, that would be all right," I said nervously.

That's where it all began.

David started calling me on the phone often. He wanted to date me. My mother objected strongly. She said I was too young so eventually I did what I felt I had to do. I would tell her I was going to a friend's house, when in reality; I was meeting up with David. It wasn't long before he told me that he loved me. And I loved him too.

I figured he must love me. When we would talk on the phone he would grill me.

David asked, "What did you do today?"

I replied, "I went bowling with my sisters."

He asked, "Just your sisters?"

"Yes."

David asked, "What were you wearing?"

"I just wore jeans and a top," I replied.

He said, "Remember no short skirt unless you're with me."

I said, "I know."

He asked, "Did any guys talk to you?"

"There was a guy talking to my sister, but not me."

"Good, I don't want you talking to any other guys. You're all mine," David said.

I said, "I know."

Yes, I thought he must surely love me. The way he wanted to know it all, every detail of my life. I became his everything and he was mine. It was intoxicating, at first. He wanted all my attention. He'd get aggravated if another guy just looked at me. He'd put his arm around me closer as if to show everyone that I was his.

I remember being at a friends' party with David. It was in their parents' basement. There was loud music and dancing and underage drinking and lots of conversations going on.

David said to me, "I'll be right back, you stay here. I'll get us a couple of more drinks."

I said, "Okay."

I was enjoying the music and watching the people who were dancing when I spotted a friend of mine walking up to me with a guy friend that I hadn't met before.

She said, "Karen, I want you to meet my friend Chuck. Chuck, this is Karen."

As Chuck offered his hand to me, he took it and pulled me closer to give me a quick hug.

"Nice to meet you, Karen."

"Hi Chuck, nice to meet you too," I said.

And as I did, I saw David walking back to us. I could see that he was pissed and without a thought, he dropped the drinks in his hands and lunged at the guy. The poor harmless guy ended up in a garbage can wondering what the hell happened!

I was speechless really and embarrassed as we were both asked to leave the home immediately.

I said, "What the hell was that about?"

He said, "I DON'T WANT ANY OTHER FUCKING GUYS TALKING TO YOU! ISN'T THAT CLEAR TO YOU BY NOW?"

"It was harmless! My friend was just introducing him to me."

"I DON'T FUCKING CARE!" he shouted. "I DON'T WANT ANYONE MESSING WITH YOU, YOU'RE MY GIRL!"

No matter what I said, he kept justifying his actions as a normal reaction.

Not wanting to spoil our whole evening together, I just let it go.

I thought that was love. Wasn't it?

Once I became old enough in my mother's eyes to date, she tried to convince me to date other boys, but my mind was already made up that David was the guy for me. We went to all the high school dances together; his and mine. We spent as much time together as possible.

David was charming. He could be so romantic. He bought me gifts all the time. He would bring me chocolates and flowers. When we would have a date, there were many times he would arrive at my house early and sit out front until it was time to pick me up. He was never late. I thought that was so sweet.

David certainly didn't want me to date anyone else so I just assumed that he and I would be together permanently with marriage sometime in the future.

I remember once when he got mad at me for something. I think maybe I had accepted a phone call from another guy and he had found out. David was two years older than me but we were both still in high school. We were in a parking lot outside a restaurant and he was really mad at me. He was yelling as he was pounding his fist on the roof of his car.

"HOW MANY FUCKING TIMES HAVE I TOLD YOU THAT I DON'T LIKE THAT? YOU HAVE FUCKING DISOBEYED ME!"

"It didn't mean anything David. He's just a friend."

"I DON'T CARE WHAT THE FUCK YOU SAY. I DON'T WANT YOU TALKING TO ANY OTHER FUCKING GUYS!" And as he pounded the top of his car some more he yelled, "DON'T EVER FUCKING DISOBEY ME AGAIN LIKE THAT! DO YOU UNDERSTAND?"

I looked around to see if there were people watching and just to make him quiet down, I said, "Okay fine, I hear you. Please stop yelling at me."

After he would lose control that way, and had time to cool off, he was full of apologies.

He'd say, "It won't happen again, I promise. If you just stay away from other guys it won't happen. I'll have no reason to get pissed off."

I'd say, "There's no reason for you to be jealous. I love you David."

I was so young and wrapped up in him that I didn't realize how controlling he had become. I confused his dominance for love.

I shook my head now to concentrate on my driving and when I arrived at the gas station, I pulled right up to the gas pump and got out of my car.

As I walked into the station, I said, "Hi Tom, could you please have one of the guys fill up my tank with gas?"

Tom said, "Sure, no problem, Karen."

I said, "Thanks, and then can you give me a hand in the office?"

"Sure, I'll be right there," said Tom.

I walked into the back office and put down my purse on the desk and pulled out the huge key ring that David normally carried with him and unlocked the top drawer of the file cabinet. I had no idea what most of the other keys opened. I pulled out the checkbook. I wanted to take care of payroll first. The business had not been doing well as of late, but the employees had to be paid. In fact they were paid before David and I were. If there was little or no money left after payroll went out, then David and I were not compensated, and we had to figure out how to get along without.

The bills at home had been piling up. I wasn't quite sure how we were ever going to catch up. And David's being away in the hospital now was not helping. It didn't matter though because I knew that he had to go into treatment. He was more likely to lose his business entirely if he didn't get help. He might even lose his life. So I hoped with all my heart that my efforts here in trying to keep things running would not end up in futility.

Tom walked into the office then and said, "Tell me Karen, how's David doing?"

Tom was the only employee at David's business that I felt that I could trust so I had told him where David really was and what we were dealing with. He'd promised to keep the information to himself and to help me out wherever he could.

I said, "He's doing okay. He's not happy where he is but I think he realizes that it's where he belongs right now, like it or not."

"When you see him next, please tell him I say hello and wish him well, okay?"

"I will Tom, thanks for asking about him. Now let's get to the payroll first."

I wrote all the checks and put them in David's briefcase, which I would take with me to the hospital. All I needed David to do was to sign them. He trusted Tom as well; he was pretty much his right hand man.

"Thanks for your help, Tom," I said.

"No problem, Karen."

"You're sure that you will be okay here tomorrow without me?"

"Yes Karen, absolutely," said Tom. "The only other thing you have to do today is the bank deposits."

"Okay, no problem," I said.

Tom went back to the car that he'd been working on as I went into the safe on the floor and pulled out all the money. I knew which percentage had to go into each account but as I counted the money over and over again I could see that we were coming up short for payroll. There was nothing else I could do but to short one account so that's what I did.

On my way out the door I said to Tom, "I will see you in a couple of days then. Call me if anything comes up, okay?"

"All right, Karen, take care."

"Thanks for all your help, Tom, you're a lifesaver!"

"You're welcome," said Tom.

I was just a couple of blocks away when my cell phone rang. It was Tom.

He said, "Karen, you left the safe open again!"

I said, "Oh crap, I'm glad you are the one that found it that way! I'm just not thinking very clearly. Did you lock it up for me?"

"Yes, I did," said Tom.

"Thank you so much, I don't know what I'd do without your help, Tom. I'll see you in a couple of days, I hope you have a good holiday," I said.

Tom said, "You too."

I made the bank deposits then and stopped home for a short visit with the kids. I had a little dinner and was out the door again with the briefcase in tow; off to the hospital to see David and to see if I could get these payroll checks signed.

When I arrived at the hospital, I took the elevator up to the floor where David was staying. I passed the nurse's station and when I walked into David's room there was no one there. I went down the hall to the family room and found that almost empty as well, except for a few family members.

I went to the front desk and asked one of the nurses, "Where is everyone? I'm looking for my husband, David."

She said, "All the patients are in group therapy right now. Please just have a seat in the family room. Your husband will be out soon to meet you."

I said, "Do you know how long he will be yet?"

"It won't be too long . . . probably about fifteen minutes. And your first therapy group with your husband starts on the hour. I hope he told you about it."

I said, "Well, no he didn't but I'm glad I'm here for it."

The nurse went on to say, "Here you go. Someone should have given you this schedule already," as she handed me a piece of paper.

I said, "Thanks, I'll take a look at this."

I walked back down the hall and took a seat in the family room and tried to focus on the schedule I'd been given. It listed all the activities for the day for the patients and their families. There were group therapy sessions listed with family, but most without, and some therapy was individual for the patient. Meal time was listed as well as exercise and down time for the patients.

I couldn't help it. *How lovely for him. So much attention. From sun up to sun down, it's all about him. What a lucky guy. While I try to muddle through the day doing his job and mine!*

I resented it. I knew that he needed all the help that he could get. But I did too.

Isn't this the way it's always been? He gets all the attention, whether it's good or bad! What about me?

As I looked around the room, I could see there were other family members looking as lost as me. I took some comfort in that. I was not alone.

Just as the nurse had promised, all the patients returned to the family room.

David smiled at me as he walked up to me and said, "Hi."

We exchanged a quick hug as I said, "How are you feeling today?"

"I'm finally starting to feel a little better physically. The medication that they are giving me seems to be taking away the fucking nausea."

"That's good. How's the therapy going?"

David said, "It's pretty eye opening! There are some people in there who are much worse off than me!"

"The nurse told me there's a family group meeting in a little while? It's a good thing I got here in time, I had no idea."

"I thought I told you. I'm sorry," said David. "My mother was here yesterday and I told her about it. She said that she hoped to make it here as well."

"Okay," I said.

A lot of help she's gonna be! Good luck with that!

David said, "Are you thirsty? I'm going to get a pop out of the fridge there, you want something?"

"I could go for a bottle of water, thanks."

As David walked by the entrance to the room to get to the fridge, he was greeted by Rita. He gave her a quick hug and she waved to me as she walked with him to get the drinks.

I stood and gave Rita a quick hug, as they walked up to me.

As they both sat down, David asked, "Where's Dad?"

"He's busy with work, he won't be able to make it tonight," said Rita.

"Oh," said David.

Liar, liar, pants on fire.

I was surprised that Rita was here at all. She really wasn't convinced that David had a problem at all and his father had never been a supportive kind of person, not ever. I wasn't surprised that he didn't show up. He saw David's addiction as a weakness that he was choosing not to control. He was obviously ashamed of his own son.

I remember the day that David and I were married. His father never spoke one word out loud to me. He never said *I love you, I hate you, you look pretty, congratulations, welcome to the family;* none of the normal things that parents say to their new daughter-in-law.

David looked up at the clock on the wall and said, "We are supposed to go to the other room now for therapy, let's go."

"Okay," I said.

You could tell as we walked into the room hesitantly that we were not the only ones who were nervous about this whole situation. Nobody looked thrilled to be here.

The group leader introduced herself first, once everyone had been seated. You could hear a pin drop as she gave a brief summation of what she hoped for all of us to accomplish in this capacity.

Betty said, "Welcome to all of you who are brave enough to be here to help your patient, your loved one, get the help they need to overcome their addictions, whatever they might be. I know it's not easy for most of you to be here. I have met all of the patients here individually and I find it to be an honor to know them all and I hope that this therapy that takes place here will be an integral part of their recovery. I'd like us now to go around the circle here and I'll ask each of you patients to introduce yourselves as well as your family members."

Each patient then introduced themselves one at a time around the circle and as it came closer to us, I could feel my palms were sweaty and my heart was beating harder. Such a foreign situation I never expected to find myself in.

David said aloud, "My name is David, and I'm an alcoholic."

"Hello David," said everyone around the circle.

"This is my wife Karen and my mother Rita."

Betty said, "Hello to you both and thanks for being here today."

I got through that first meeting somehow.

Betty kept telling all of us how much work it would require on all of our parts to help our patient to be healthy again. She suggested that we as family members find our own support groups as well. She suggested that Al -Anon groups could be beneficial to us. The more she talked about all the work that his recovery would require, the more aggravated I felt.

This is his problem, not mine! He created this crap, not me. He's the sick one. I don't have enough shit to do? I have to go to all sorts of meetings? I don't think so. I just don't have it in me. I'm already running on empty!

I was not feeling at all receptive to all the work that lay ahead for me in David's recovery; not that day anyway.

Once the meeting let out, Rita said goodbye. David walked her to the elevator. I felt so weary by this time of the day. I just wanted David to sign these checks in the briefcase and get home and crash.

We managed to do that without incident.

I said to David, "I won't be able to visit tomorrow, there's no one to watch the kids and I'm exhausted. I need a day at home."

I didn't feel the need to share with him that I was having some family over to try to celebrate New Year's Eve.

I'm too weary to even talk.

He frowned and said, "It gets lonely here."

"Please don't make me feel guilty. I have to be home with the kids tomorrow," I said.

I just want to go home.

"I guess that's okay," David said.

"I'll be back on New Year's Day. Kim said she will come over to spend time with the kids," I said.

Just let me out of here. I feel like I'm suffocating!

"Okay," said David, "I'll walk you out."

I couldn't even look back at him as I walked out the hospital door where I left him. I thought I might scream.

How will I get through this?

I got into my car, turned on the headlights and turned the radio on full blast so that I couldn't hear the thoughts inside my head.

CHAPTER 6

I WOKE UP ON NEW Year's Eve feeling relieved that I could stay home this day. I was up before the kids stirred and decided to make them their favorite breakfast.

It never failed. I was halfway through cooking the pound of bacon when all their sleepy little heads appeared.

I said with a smile, "Happy New Year's Eve to all of you! Get over here, all of you! I need a group hug! We are having a party today!"

All three came running up to me and just about knocked me to the floor as they remembered that we would have company over today. Their hugs were so comforting.

"Yippee!" all three of them laughed with delight.

"Go watch some cartoons now, and I'll call you when the pancakes are ready."

I'd always found cooking to be therapeutic for me. It always made me feel accomplished to serve good food to my family and this day was no different. It helped me to take my mind off all the crap I was dealing with. I just wanted to forget it all and enjoy my kids today.

The day flew by. I did a little cleaning and some laundry and caught up on the mail. I got the kids all bathed in the afternoon after Valerie's nap and got them all dressed for the evening celebration. I braided the girls' hair which they loved and matched the bows in their hair to the outfits they wore.

David called me from the hospital late in the afternoon in a terrible mood.

He said, "I don't know if I can make it through this fucking treatment. I feel like fucking shit. I just want to leave here. And why haven't you called me all fucking day? There's nothing to do here today because of the fucking holiday."

I said, "I've been busy with the kids today and I've been trying to catch up around the house."

"It's New Year's Eve. I should be there with you and the kids today," he said.

"David, that's not what we agreed to. You said that you would stay there for the thirty day program."

"But it's the holiday," he moaned.

I said, "It really doesn't matter what day it is, David . . . you know you need to be there. I'll give Denny a call and I'll ask him to call you there. Maybe that would help you out?"

He said, "Are you seriously not coming to see me today?"

"I told you yesterday that I have to be here with the kids. I will see you tomorrow."

"Okay, whatever!"

"I'll talk to you tomorrow David. I love you."

The phone went dead then. He hung up on me. I stared at the phone in my hand.

The nerve of him! Is he for real? I'm the one who should be pissed off here! It's your fault that you are there! The mess that we are in is all your fault!

I thought all these things but would not say them out loud. Not to him anyway, for fear of his reaction. I never really could express my feelings with David. He'd convinced me that my feelings were stupid and insignificant. The only thing that mattered were his feelings. My world and his revolved around him alone. He made sure to make his feelings very clear about that.

I gave up a long time ago trying to express myself to him because he didn't care enough to listen. I gave up. I kept it all inside.

I took a deep breath and waited a couple of minutes to slow my racing heart and went back to preparing a few things before our guests arrived for the party.

The doorbell rang and J.R. shouted, "They're here, Mom!"

All my family arrived within minutes of each other. It felt so good to have them all with me.

Nancy hugged me and said, 'Thanks for having us over, Karen! Let's get this party started!"

My brother Ken said, "Are you okay, Karen? And how's David?"

"I'm doing all right and David's doing all right but he's a long way from being well. And if you don't mind, I'm going to try to talk about other things tonight. I need to get my mind off of him for a little while, okay?"

As he hugged me he said, "Sure Sis, whatever you need."

J.R. and his cousins stayed upstairs to play with his toys, and the rest of us went downstairs to the family room. I turned on the music and tried to get lost in conversation.

Everyone seemed to be having fun. Some of us were dancing to the music. It felt so good to try to focus on something other than David.

When I hung up the phone with the pizza place, my phone rang again. It was David.

He said, "What are you doing?"

I said, "My sisters and brothers are here to keep me company. The kids are playing with their cousins."

I could hear him seething as he said, "I can't believe you are not here. All the other patients have their family here and where are you? Living it up with your family!"

"I told you several times that I could not be there today. I needed a bit of normalcy today. I needed one day at home. I told you that!"

David said, "You say you care about me, you are full of shit!" His voice got louder, "IF YOU CARED, YOU WOULD BE HERE!"

All I could hear then was the phone hanging up in my ear again. I'm sure I must have looked upset because as soon as I hung up the phone, Nancy said, "Karen, what's wrong? Are you okay?"

I couldn't help the tears that welled in my eyes as I said, "That was David and now he's mad at me because I am not there at the hospital with him. I told him I just needed one day at home. He's trying to make me feel guilty."

Nancy said, "Screw him Karen! You need to take care of yourself! Not just him anymore! Don't let him make you feel guilty!"

"I know you're right. It's about time I think of myself for a change. This is going to be a rough month, I can see that!"

As Nancy hugged me she said, "Whenever it gets to be too much for you, call me. I can't be over here a lot to help because I have the kids at home too, but anytime you need to talk just call me, promise?"

"I promise," I said.

As we all ate pizza a little later, my phone rang again. It was David.

He yelled, "I'VE DECIDED I'M NOT STAYING IN THIS FUCKING PLACE AND I WANT YOU TO COME AND GET ME RIGHT FUCKING NOW!"

With a lump in my throat but being braver because he was not there next to me I said, "No, I can't do that."

"YOU BITCH!" He screamed at me, "I SAID COME AND GET ME NOW!"

I said with more courage than I thought I ever had, "No, I will not do that! You can call one of your drinking buddies or your druggie friends to come and get you. I will not pick you up!"

This time I hung up on him.

Within minutes he called again and screamed at me, "THIS IS THE LAST FUCKING TIME I'M GOING TO TELL YOU TO GET IN THE FUCKING CAR AND FUCKING COME AND GET ME RIGHT FUCKING NOW!"

"And for the last time," I said, "I'm telling you that I will do no such thing. And if you decide to leave there, do not come home. I will call the police and have you removed! You may not come back to this house unless you follow through with treatment there!"

He said, "WHO THE FUCK DO YOU THINK YOU'RE TALKING TO? THAT'S MY HOUSE!"

I said, "It's my house as well and I will do whatever it takes to keep the kids and myself safe! Please don't call here again today. I will not come and get you. I can't. I will see you there tomorrow."

David hung up on me again. The phone rang a couple of more times but I didn't pick it up again. I muted the ring and figured that was all I could do for today. I had to ignore him. There was no way that I could allow him back into the house.

It wouldn't be safe for me or the kids. All I could do was pray that he would stay where he was. All I could do was hope that he would stay for the therapy that he needed to start his life again, sober.

Fortunately, David decided to stay where he was. He didn't threaten to leave treatment again. I believe in his heart he knew that he needed help in a big way.

The holidays passed. I got into a routine of sorts where I'd go to the gas station every day and do what needed to be done, stop at home to check on the kids, and go to the hospital every evening to support David as best I could. It was draining to say the least.

And as promised the therapy at the hospital became intense.

David seemed very free to admit to many things that he had been doing that I was totally unaware of.

It was the norm in a group therapy session for the focus to be on a couple of patients and their family members. This night, dreadfully so, they focused on David and me.

There were about fifteen people in the group tonight. It looked like five were family members. The rest were patients.

Betty asked, "Have you admitted yet to your wife all the things that you have been involved in for the last couple of years, David? Have you told her the things that you have admitted to me?"

David said, "No, I haven't."

She said, "You know that following the steps of the program include being honest and up front to everyone, especially your family, yes?"

"Yes," he said.

Betty said, "Are you ready to be totally honest with Karen so that you can wipe the slate clean and have a new beginning?"

"I am," David said quietly.

I could hardly breathe as he began to speak.

"I've been lying to you, Karen. I admit now that I've been at the bar far more often than I'd told you and I can't control my liquor."

All eyes were on me now. I could hardly speak as he looked at me for my reaction.

"I knew that," I managed to say.

"There's more," he said. "You were right about your suspicions about my using drugs. I started using cocaine about a year ago."

I could hardly see across the room for the tears that were welling in my eyes as he went on to say. "I've been selling cocaine too . . . out of the gas station. My partner found out what I was doing. That's why he wanted out."

I'm sure my face was red because it felt so hot. I clasped my fingers together in my lap and could feel how sweaty my hands had become.

For a moment there was dead silence in the room.

Oh my God! Who is this guy? Is this my husband? Dealing drugs?

Betty said, "Karen, do you have questions for David?"

I said, "I'm so shocked right now . . . I can't think. I'm sure I will have questions but not now. No."

How could you do this? What kind of person are you? Who are you?

Betty said, "David, is there anything else you want to share with Karen now?"

"No," said David.

Oh my God! Please move on. Stop looking at me. Pick on someone else.

Much to my relief, Betty moved on to another patient. Mark had apparently tried smuggling in a bottle of pain pills upon admission to the hospital. In front of the group, he admitted this to his mom who was sitting next to him. Mark was only about eighteen years old.

I'd been told by David that upon admission to the floor, each patient's bags were inspected for anything suspicious. The reality of this whole ordeal was hitting me like a ton of bricks. I suppose for David it must have been a bit like a jail sentence.

You're lucky you aren't in jail! Maybe you should be!

For the rest of the session I was totally zoned out. I could see people's mouths moving as they spoke but I really didn't hear a word because my heart was pounding so loudly. A couple of times as I glanced at David who was sitting next to me, I was surprised to see just how calm he seemed, when I just wanted to jump out of my skin. I wanted to run out of the room screaming. I wanted this meeting to be over so I could try to digest what I'd heard from David and figure out how the hell to get past it!

I managed to go through the motions of looking like I was listening to everyone who spoke for the remainder of the session, until it was finally over.

As we walked out of the meeting I said to David, "I have to head home now. Dolores asked me to get home by eight o'clock. She needs to be somewhere else. I have to get home to the kids."

In reality there was no hurry to get home.

If I don't get out of here now, I'm going to explode into pieces!

David said, "I wanted to talk to you more about the session and what was talked about."

"It will have to wait until tomorrow. Let me try to absorb everything I heard, okay?"

They will have to sweep up all the bits of me!

David said, "Okay, I'll walk you out then."

I was so used to holding all my feelings inside for fear of the results that I managed to walk down the hall without *detonating*.

My car was parked in the lot very near the door that David stood at, as he watched me walk to my car. I didn't look back at him as I slid into the driver's seat and turned on the headlights. I couldn't look back.

I turned the key in the ignition knowing that he was watching me. I put the car into gear and pulled away from the hospital. I drove a couple of blocks away and stopped the car near a school on a side street.

I didn't even realize that tears were streaming down my face. I felt like someone was strangling me. I was sad and furious and shocked all at the same time. I couldn't drive home just yet. I was shocked that all the things that I had suspected about David and what he was up to were true. I didn't want them to be true but I knew in my heart that they were.

Why then did I feel like such a fool now? How could I not have known what the hell he was doing for sure? How many other people know? How stupid do they think I am for not knowing? I felt blinded by his deceit!

As it all began to sink in I felt terrified.

What kind of shady people has he been dealing with? Does he owe them money or drugs? Now that David is in the hospital, will they show up at my doorstep wanting what they are owed? Will the kids and I be safe? How could he do this to us? Oh my God! How will I live through all of this?

I felt sick to my stomach as I put the car into gear and drove home.

CHAPTER 7

THE NEXT COUPLE OF WEEKS of David's treatment went by in a blur. I was so busy running from the house to the gas station and back to the hospital that I was anxious for it all to be over so that I could get back to my life. I hated being away from my kids so much. My biggest goal in life as a mom was to help my children to become healthy and happy and loving contributing members of this big world we live in, and no one could do that better than me.

As I listened to the conversations going on in group therapy, I began to see that I needed help as well. Rita showed up for one more meeting after that first one and I think she felt insulted with some of the conversations going on. There was talk about how addiction and the behavior that goes along with it, all runs in families. They talked about how each family member plays their role in allowing the dysfunction to continue unless someone changes something. She too had been embroiled in the disease of alcoholism for all of her life. She had an alcoholic father, brother, and sister; all of them having passed away from alcohol related illnesses. I guess it all hit too close to home for her and she wasn't about to admit that she needed to change anything.

I realized more and more how affected I'd been from David's addictions. I knew that in order for me to become a better parent that I needed to examine my own behavior. I needed to start thinking about myself and what I could do to be better. I'd been so involved with David and only David that I'd lost sight of everything else. Even with as busy as I'd been, being without David at home these past couple of weeks had given me a chance to take a look at myself. It had given me a chance to take a breath and to begin to think about what I might want in this lifetime for myself.

I knew then, that I was going to do whatever I could to make changes in my life to improve not only my marriage to David but even more importantly to better myself; and in turn benefit my children. I wasn't sure how, but I knew this had to be done.

I'd gotten the phone number from Betty for my local Al-Anon office so that I could find a group in my neighborhood. I thought that as soon as David got back home that I would call the help line and get myself to a meeting. I still resented it but knew that I needed it badly.

This whole situation that I'd found myself in now pretty much sucked. It made me sad. It made me angry. This sure as shit wasn't what I'd thought of as my happily ever after . . . far from it! I was afraid, but I thought I could muster up the courage to go to a meeting. I was willing to try anything to change some things in my life. I just wanted to feel better. I was tired of feeling miserable and scared. I was always on edge.

I brought the kids to the hospital a couple of times to visit their dad. Sunday was the day when most of the family members would visit.

We were all in the family gathering room one Sunday. The room was crowded with patients and their families. There actually seemed to be a lightness in the air that I hadn't felt in a long time. The TV was blaring on one end of the room and at the other was a pool table. David was playing a game with one of his roommates. There were some board games on a table in the middle of the room and J.R. was on the floor playing checkers with Mark. Mark behaved like a kid himself. It broke my heart to think of how difficult his recovery would be for him and his family. It was hard enough dealing with a husband's addiction. I imagined that it would be even more difficult with a child.

It made me laugh as I watched them get playful. I was getting some juice for the girls when I heard a commotion coming from where J.R. was playing. He had taken a deck of cards and was throwing them up as far as he could over his head and he was allowing them to rain down all over himself. My first impulse was to shout at him to stop but what happened was so much better. Mark picked up another deck and began throwing them as well and one by one every person in the room began to notice. Everyone began to laugh. The room roared with laughter.

Mark and J.R. picked up the cards again and again and threw them all over the place. Now that they had an audience, they laughed even harder and so did I. I laughed so hard that the tears rolled down my face. I told myself that I should get J.R. to stop but I just couldn't; I was paralyzed with laughter. I felt almost crazy with the way that I was laughing. My stomach began to hurt from laughing so hard.

Oh my God, am I losing my mind?

The laughter around the room started to subside . . . except for mine. With the laughter, I felt such a huge release of anxiety. It felt so good to laugh about such a simple little thing . . . and to laugh so hard that I cried.

And as I laughed like a lunatic it hit me again, all of a sudden. As I looked into the faces around the room that were all looking back at me I had that ah-ha moment once again.

I'm NOT alone! Thank you God, I'm not alone!

All these people around me were dealing with the same kinds of things as me. I'd felt so all alone in my despair for so long that it was such a huge relief to finally know that I was not alone. There is strength in numbers for sure, and finally I felt a bit of a camaraderie being in this same room, with other people who must have some of the same feelings as me. We were all in this together.

At last, the day for David to come home had arrived. I was nervous to say the least. It had been calm in my home for a month and I didn't want that to change. I was hopeful. I truly believed that now that David and I had the tools to recover that we would both work at changing what we needed to in order to become a healthy family.

When I arrived at the hospital that final day, David was ready to go. I went up to his room to help him carry some of his things out.

He gave me a hug as he said, "I can't wait to get the hell out of here. I just want to go home."

"I know, David. Have you got everything?"

Just then Betty poked her head into the doorway and said, "Good luck to you both! Don't forget they will be expecting you in your after care group meeting in two days."

I said, "Oh wow, I didn't realize that it starts so soon."

Betty said, "No time like the present. We want to make sure that neither one of you forgets what you've only just begun to learn here. You are going to love your group leaders . . . they're great! They are a couple themselves. Their names are Keith and Debbie."

David said, "I actually met Keith at one of the AA meetings I was at a couple of days ago. He seems to be an okay kinda guy."

"He's great!" said Betty.

Betty stood in between us and put her arms around us both then and said, "You two can come back and visit anytime. I'd love to see how you are doing. I truly mean that. Good luck!"

"Thanks Betty," I said. "It's been good working with you. Thanks for all your help."

"It's been my pleasure working with you and David. He reminds me of a big ole teddy bear," she said.

David laughed as he gave her a hug and said, "Thanks for everything Betty, maybe I'll see you around at a meeting."

That was likely since Betty was a recovering addict herself.

"I hope so," said Betty.

We walked down the hall then. David dragged his suitcase in one hand and held mine in the other.

As we came to the exit door, I was fooled again by the sunshine. It was beating down on the snow so brightly that you would have thought it was not so cold out. But as we opened the door, I gasped as the cold wind hit me; taking my breath away.

As we walked to the car, I said, "I can drive if you want."

David said, "No, I haven't driven in a month, let me."

"Okay," I said.

As we drove home, we talked about a lot of things. There was so much to catch up on. While David was in the hospital, he'd had a complete health work up and through some blood work had been newly diagnosed as diabetic. He was not at all happy with that and seemed to be going through some denial.

"Did Betty give you the name of the doctor she wants you to see for your diabetes follow up?"

"I think I have it somewhere."

I said, "This diabetes stuff is pretty serious, isn't it?"

David said, "I'm hoping that it will go away. They said it's possible that my body is in shock from the drugs and alcohol and that maybe things will even out with a little time."

"I hope so too, but it doesn't seem very likely, does it?"

David said, "I really don't want to talk about that right now. I want to get home, see the kids and get back to work and see what kind of fucking mess I have to deal with there."

I raised my eyebrows and sighed as I said, "Okay, we can talk about it later."

"Thank you," he said. "I just want to get back into a normal routine again."

"I understand. I am definitely marking the calendar though for those after care meetings every Wednesday. We need to go."

"Yeah, that's fine."

The kids were happy to see their dad at home again even though I could see their hesitancy to get too close to him for fear of his reaction. Kids are incredibly perceptive, and even at their young ages they were so smart. They had witnessed David at his worst, but because I always seemed to forgive him, they followed my example and did the same.

David was anxious to get back to work so after unpacking his suitcase he said, "I'm going to take off now. I'll probably be late getting back home. I'm sure there's lots of stuff for me to take care of at the station."

"Okay," I said, "I'll save you some dinner. Don't be eating junk food. You know what the doctor said."

He gave me a hug and kissed me and said, "Yeah, yeah, I know. I'll see you later."

I said, "I love you, David."

"I love you too."

CHAPTER 8

I HAVE TO ADMIT THAT every time David went out the door after that I was nervous. I worried about so many things. I wondered whether he would be able to handle being back in the same situations where he used to drink and do drugs and be able to control his behaviors.

Can he be around the same people and not fall into the same habits? Is that even possible? Have I done enough at the gas station to keep it alive and thriving?

And then I remembered something I had heard in therapy. I needed to put the focus back on me. I had no control over David and his behavior. That had been made perfectly clear! The only person I could control was myself.

I needed to take care of me for a change. I needed to think of myself first because I needed to be healthy in my mind in order for anything else in my life to be right. I needed to have a clear head to be the best parent that I could be, and I hoped that if I worked on that, that all the other parts of my life would fall into place just like dominoes.

I called the number that Betty had given me for the Al-Anon help line. I said to the person who picked up, "I need to find a meeting in my neighborhood, can you help me?"

"I'd be happy to help you," she said. "There's actually several that are not too far from you. Here are the places and times."

As I finished writing down the information she gave me I said, "I've never been to a meeting. Can you tell me a little bit about what I can expect? How long are they usually? I'll need to let my babysitter know how long I'll be."

She said, "Each meeting runs about an hour and a half. I suggest that you try several meetings before you decide if it's for you or not. Don't decide after just one meeting because you are going to meet different people at each one, and that will make each meeting different from the next."

I said, "What do they do at these meetings?"

She said, "Al-Anon members do not give direction or advice to other members. Instead they share their personal experiences and stories, and invite other members to take what they like and leave the rest . . . that is to determine for themselves what lessons they can apply to their own lives."

"Do I have to speak?"

She said, "No, you can certainly just listen if you want to. You will learn how to apply the principles of the Al-Anon program to meet your needs. You will learn that you are not alone in the problems you are facing and you will realize that you have choices that can lead to a greater peace of mind whether your alcoholic chooses to drink or not."

I said, "Thanks so much for your help."

She said, "If you find that none of the meetings I've given you work out, please be sure to call us back for help."

"Great," I said. "I will."

"And when you get to the meetings, make sure that you check out some of the free literature that they all carry. You will find all sorts of helpful information in those brochures as well."

"Thanks again," I said.

I planned on going to a meeting the next week as long as I was able to arrange for a sitter.

I talked to David about my planning on attending meetings.

"I found a couple of Al-Anon meetings right in our neighborhood. I plan on going to one next week to try it out," I said.

David said, "You really think that you need to go?"

I shook my head as I said, "Didn't you hear what was said at the hospital? Your recovery is more likely if I get help as well! I'm going to do it for me and for you and for the kids!"

"Oh . . . okay if that's what you want," David said dismissively.

"Have you found any AA meetings for yourself yet?"

David said, "I've been so busy with work since I got home that I haven't had time to do that yet."

"You need to do it soon, David. How can you expect to stay sober if you don't do the things that were suggested to you in treatment?"

He said, "Don't fucking tell me what to do! I'll get there when I'm ready!"

"Okay whatever, but remember our first after care group is tomorrow night. We need to be there at seven o'clock."

David said, "I'm not sure if I can leave the gas station by then. I don't know if I can make it."

"David! You promised that you were going to attend with me! Your sister Kim has promised me that she can be here every Wednesday to watch the kids so don't even give me that crap now! We need to be there!"

"What the fuck . . . FINE!!"

I was glad now that Kim had promised to help because if we had anyone else watching the kids it would have been easier for David to back out. She knew where we were going and now that most of our family members knew what was going on with us, many of them would have been glad to speak up if they knew that David wasn't doing what he should.

I was so happy to be home again with the kids. You know how they say that you don't know what you miss until it's gone? That's exactly how I felt. I was so grateful to be able to do my full time job again taking care of my three beautiful children. I reveled in the car pooling, the housework, and the shopping, and playing with the kids. I loved it all and knew that I was lucky to be home with them.

J.R. was in kindergarten so I'd drive him back and forth to school after I'd pack them all up into the car. I took him to his after school activities as well. J.R. was such an active kid who had a tendency to get himself into trouble if he wasn't kept busy enough; so I kept him busy! I'd watch him in his Tae Kwan Do classes in the winter and I'd take him to his T-Ball games in the summer. The girls were always with me wherever we went. People hardly recognized us if we weren't together; like the four amigos we were.

Wednesday night came and David was just out of the shower as Kim arrived right on time at the front door.

"Hi Kim, thanks for being here. I really appreciate it."

"No problem, Karen. I'm happy I can do something to help you guys out. I know you have your hands full here."

The kids came running when they heard their aunt's voice.

"Aunt Kim!" they all yelled collectively, as they ran from out of their rooms to hug her.

Kim always came to the house bearing gifts for the kids and today was no different. She had a new movie for J.R. to watch and a couple of new books to read to the girls. She helped to make them all feel very special. It really does take a village. The more people who are involved with helping to raise your children the better. The more people who they love, the more well-rounded a child becomes.

Gina and Valerie had already piled up all the books that they wanted Kim to read to them. She sat down on the couch with a smile and said, "We'd better get started, that's a lot of books!"

I gave them all a hug goodbye and we were off to our first after care group (ACG).

There was not a lot of conversation on our drive to the meeting. David had seemed so touchy since he'd gotten home from the hospital. Every time I tried to bring something of importance up, he'd get mad at me. I thought surely the subject of what he was doing to begin his recovery would come up at the meeting.

I said, "How's everything going at the gas station?"

"Not very good. I had a meeting today with the big boss from the company where we purchase our gas. You know the fucking asshole that you had to deal with!"

"I know who you are talking about, yes," I said. "I had to lie to him about where you've been for the last month. He took me out to lunch at the restaurant next to your gas station. He tried to pry it out of me but I told him you had issues going on with your diabetes. I tried to be as vague as I could be."

David replied, "I know that you did the best that you could Karen. He's such an asshole. I can't stand the guy! He's trying to tell me how to run my fucking business."

"I'm sorry it's not going well." I said.

"If I can't work things out with him, I'll have no fucking gasoline to sell and I'll be out of business before you know it."

"I know you're facing a lot now but you have to try to put your recovery first or you'll have nothing anyway," I said.

David said, "I know! I know! I have so much on my mind! I can't fucking think!"

As we drove up to the town hall where the meetings were held, David seemed to calm down a bit. When we got inside, there was a group of people milling around, chatting with one another. David spoke to a couple of them that he recognized from the hospital. He introduced me to a few. He was always on his best behavior in front of other people. He was such a performer. Just a minute before the meeting was to start; we all filed into the room and sat in a large circle of chairs. There were fourteen of us there including the group leaders. They introduced themselves.

A nice looking middle aged man with dark hair that was graying around the temples said, "Welcome to all of you. My name is Keith and right next to me here is Debbie. She is the co-leader here as well as my girlfriend. I'm a recovering alcoholic myself. I've been sober now for three years. My drug of choice was vodka. I'd like us to first go around the group here and ask you each to introduce yourselves and tell us who you are with. Can you start us off Debbie?"

"I sure can," she said with a southern drawl.

I could see that Debbie was quite a bit younger than Keith. Her blonde hair was pulled up in the back of her head with a comb of sorts and she wore a cute little skirt with flat, black comfortable looking shoes.

"My name is Debbie," she said with a little giggle, "like Keith said. Keith and I have been a couple for about two and a half years, so I didn't know him through the worst part of his addiction, but I come from a background of addiction. I have several family members who have suffered from addictions of one kind or another. I've actually been active in Al-Anon for about five years now."

I was sitting next to Debbie so I was next in line to introduce myself.

I said, "My name is Karen and I'm here to support my husband," as I looked in his direction.

David then said, "My name is David and I just got out of treatment a few days ago. I have thirty three days of sobriety so far. My drugs of choice were scotch and cocaine."

As we went around the room with introductions, I recognized a few of the people from the hospital but there were new faces as well.

Young Mark was there with his brother to support him. There was a friendly looking young couple around our same ages. Their names were Pam and Dan. Pam was pregnant she said, with their first child and she was afraid of whether the baby was going to be healthy or not because of her husband's using drugs when she became pregnant.

There was another couple whose names were Jeff and Marie. Jeff had been addicted to alcohol for twenty some years. His wife Marie had been plagued with epileptic seizures for about the same duration as Jeff's addiction. It seemed that her seizures were sometimes brought on with the stress and worry that goes along with living with an addict.

After everyone had talked a little about themselves, Keith said, "All of you have been in some kind of treatment center in different facilities around this area. The purpose of this group is to help you all adjust to your new drug free lives. We hope to help you overcome your addictions permanently. It's not an easy journey to take and we hope that these meetings will give you the courage that it will take to be successful in your recoveries . . . for the addicted person as well as the family members. We want to offer you the necessary tools to achieve success."

Debbie chimed in then and said, "I've lived with addicted people for all of my life and I knew for a long time that I needed help for myself to learn how to react differently to difficult circumstances. I was miserable. There's a saying that goes, *'If you keep on doing what you've always done, you'll keep on getting what you've always gotten.'* In fact, I've realized that when I react differently to my addict, sometimes the end result can be totally different from what it used to be before I started to work on myself. I have been working the steps of Al-Anon for a few years now and all I can tell you is that I feel good. I feel better emotionally than I have in years."

As I listened to Debbie, I felt already like I could relate to her. Some of the things she talked about were a bit foreign to me. Working the steps? I wasn't sure what she meant by that, but I had a feeling that a lot of things would become clear to me in this very room.

Keith started asking questions randomly. He asked, "Mark, how many AA meetings have you been to since you were released from the hospital?"

Mark said, "I got out five days ago and I've been to two meetings every day."

His brother who sat next to him put his arm around Mark's shoulders and patted him on the back saying, "Nice going Bro! I'm proud of you."

Keith said, "That's great Mark. Keep it up."

Debbie said, "Karen, how are you?"

Oh my God, why did you pick me? Do I look as freaked out and uncomfortable as I feel?

"I'm okay," I said timidly.

Debbie said, "Have you considered Al-Anon for yourself yet?"

"I did make a phone call and I got the places and times written down at home. I have plans on getting to a meeting this upcoming week."

She said, "That's great. I'd like to hear about it next week when we see you here. I'd like to know what you think, okay?"

I said, "Sure."

Keith said, "David, you've been quiet over there. How's it been for you? How many meetings have you been to since your release?"

David said, "I was just at one last night and I have a couple more lined up in the next couple of days."

Oh my God! You fucking liar!

"What was your first impression? Do you think it may help you to stay on the right path?" asked Keith.

"Yeah, it was okay. I think it may help," said David.

Oh my God, what a bold faced lie! How do you do that with a straight face?

Keith said, "Once you've got a couple more meetings under your belt, we'd like to hear more about how you think it's helping you. Does that sound good?"

"Sure," said David. And as he turned my way he had that look on his face that said, you better not say anything! I knew that look too well so I didn't dare contradict what he'd said.

What good is this going to do anyone if you are going to lie through it all?

I wanted to scream at him but of course I didn't.

Another hour went by as Keith and Debbie tried to make us all feel a little more comfortable by asking questions of all of us, so that in upcoming meetings we'd be more likely to start sharing the real issues that we were all facing in one way or another, with attempted recovery.

At the close of the meeting we all stood and said the Serenity Prayer together.

"God grant me the serenity to accept the things I cannot change, courage to change the things I can, and wisdom to know the difference."

Before we left, everyone milled around a bit in the foyer. Debbie came right up to me and said, "Karen, can I give you a hug? You look like you can use one."

I smiled and said, "Sure, you know I could use a hug."

"I look forward to getting to know you better. I've been where you are, and I know it doesn't feel good right now but it will get better as long as you are willing to make some changes," Debbie said in that adorable southern drawl.

Her accent alone made me smile.

I said, "Thanks Debbie, your support means a lot."

David was just saying goodbye to Mark and with a strained smile on his face as he saw who I was talking to, he walked up to me and said, "You ready to go?"

"Sure, I'm ready. I'll see you next week Debbie," I said.

"Bye bye, Karen, see you next week David," said Debbie.

It was snowing outside when we got into the car. It was windy and the snow was that mixture of snowflakes and pelting ice that you just dread when you have to drive in it for any distance. We shivered in the car until there was finally heat enough to turn the defrosters on so that the windows would clear enough to see where we were going.

I said to David, "So what do you think? How do you feel about the meeting?"

David said, "I think its total bullshit! I'm a grown man! They think they are going to fucking tell me what to do?"

Seriously? I thought as I shook my head slowly back and forth.

David got out of the car to scrape the remaining snow and ice off the windshield. When he got back in, he put the car into drive, turned the heat up, and headed in the direction of our house.

"That's really the impression you got?" I asked.

"Yeah, it is! Didn't you?"

I said, "No, I feel like the two of them have been in recovery long enough to be able to suggest to us what worked for them. I think it's generous of them to share what they have learned in the hopes of helping us as well. And I liked Debbie right away. I feel like I can relate to her."

David said, "I think that Keith talked like a fucking know-it all. I felt like he talked down to me."

"Wow," I said, "I didn't get that feeling at all."

David said, "Well I did. I don't know if that group is going to be any help to me at all."

"It's the first time we went! Give it a chance. Why in the world did you lie to him about going to a meeting?"

David said, "I couldn't tell him that I haven't gone yet. He would have been all over me. I don't need him fucking judging me!"

I said, "I don't understand why you can't be honest! Isn't lying one of the things that's gotten you into so much trouble?"

"FUCK YOU! Don't you be judging me either. I'll say whatever the fuck I want to say whenever the fuck I want to."

"I just think that you're defeating the purpose of us going to these meetings if you are going to lie," I said.

David screamed at me, "IF YOU DON'T LIKE IT, YOU KNOW WHAT? YOU CAN JUST GET THE FUCK OUT OF THIS CAR RIGHT NOW!"

As he yelled at me he drove faster and I was already nervous about us being out in this weather so for now I said nothing more.

Chapter 9

THE KIDS AND I WERE once again in the small front foyer of our little brick bungalow as he raged through the house again like a hurricane.

It had started out innocently enough when I'd asked David, "Have you set up an AA meeting for yourself yet?"

David yelled at me, "I WANT YOU TO STOP FUCKING BOTHERING ME ABOUT THAT! I HAVE SO MUCH TO DO AT THE GAS STATION! I DON'T HAVE TIME FOR THAT FUCKING SHIT! JUST LEAVE ME THE FUCK ALONE!"

The kids had been watching TV but all three came into the kitchen where David and I were to see if I was okay. I could see from the looks on their faces that they were scared.

David yelled, "ALL OF YOU GO INTO YOUR ROOMS, THIS IS BETWEEN YOUR MOTHER AND ME!"

But the girls clung to my legs as David knocked everything off of the kitchen counter with one fell swoop of his arm. J.R.'s school papers were there along with my full cup of coffee. He hit it with such force that the coffee splattered all over the wall across the room. The cup was in a hundred pieces on the floor.

Oh shit! Here we go again!

As quickly as I could, I put my arms around the girls, who were crying by now and pushed them along with me in the direction of the front of the house into the foyer by the front door.

I said to J.R., "Come with me, quick!"

As we ran to the front of the house David yelled, "I FUCKING HATE MY LIFE AND THIS HOUSE AND YOU!"

I could hear him pick up his keys and throw them in the direction of the refrigerator. I heard them make contact . . . hard!

David yelled, "NOBODY IS GOING TO FUCKING TELL ME WHAT TO DO! I DON'T HAVE TO PUT UP WITH THIS! WHO THE FUCK DO YOU THINK YOU ARE?"

By this time I'd pushed all the kids behind me in the small foyer, and I stood in front of them to protect them.

If we have to, we can run out the front door.

I could see David around the corner. His face was as red as it could be when he tore one of the pictures off the wall in the hallway and threw it in our direction. I could see it fall to the floor in pieces after it left a new dent in the wall.

"I DON'T NEED THIS BULLSHIT!" he screamed in my direction. "I MAY AS WELL GO OUT AND DRINK! I FELT MUCH BETTER THEN!"

As he came closer to us, into the living room, I held my arms out wide and held the kids safe behind me.

David ran right up to me and spit in my face as he screamed again, "I HATE YOU AND THIS FUCKING HOUSE AND MY LIFE! I MAY AS WELL BE DEAD! DO YOU HEAR ME?"

"I can hear you. Stop shouting, your scaring the kids," I said.

David raised his fist in front of my face then.

"DADDY! STOP!" yelled J.R., as he dared to poke his little head out from behind me.

David was so lost in his delirium that he didn't even seem to hear J.R. or the girls crying for that matter.

"David! You don't mean that. You're scaring the kids! STOP!"

Oh my God, please just get the hell out of here! Leave!

"HOW MANY TIMES DO I HAVE TO TELL YOU TO STOP FUCKING TELLING ME WHAT TO DO? THIS IS ALL YOUR FAULT! YOU BROUGHT THIS ON YOURSELF, YOU BITCH!"

I lowered my head as he screamed at me some more, all the while my arms outstretched to keep the kids behind me.

My heart is going to burst right out of my chest!

"I DON'T HAVE TO STAY HERE AND TOLERATE THIS BULLSHIT!" David yelled.

With that he turned away from us and marched back into the kitchen. I watched as he threw on his coat, picked up his keys and his cigarettes and walked out the back door. He slammed the door so hard that the whole house shook. I heard glass shattering.

Thank God! He's leaving!

I waited for just a minute to make sure he didn't come back. I heard the garage door close as he drove away.

His tantrum through the house seemed to last for an eternity when in reality it was just a couple of minutes. A couple of minutes of terror for me and the kids.

This was how he controlled us all.

As I took a deep breath, I put my arms around the kids and directed them to the couch where we all sat down. I realized as I began to try to calm them down that my face was wet with tears.

Gina sat next to me as close as she could. She could hardly catch her breath from crying as she asked, "Why is Daddy so mad at you?"

What do I say?

My arms were shaking as I hugged her and said, "He's really not mad at me. I know it's hard to believe but he's just not feeling good. He's feeling kind of sick and we have to try to help him feel better."

J.R. said, "I thought he would be better after he was in the hospital!"

I said, "So did I, but I guess it's going to take longer than we thought."

J.R. puffed out his chest with tears in his eyes as he said, "I hate him!"

I said, "No, you don't really. You're mad at him. I don't blame you. He's so wrong for behaving the way that he is."

I hugged Valerie as she sat in my lap and I wiped her tears with a tissue. "You're safe now, Sweetie. It's okay."

J.R. said, "I do hate him, Mom. He's scaring you and the girls. I hate him."

I said, "It's okay for you to feel that way right now. I hope that it will pass."

I think I hate him too.

Gina said, "I love you, Mommy."

"I know you do and I love all of you. Now how about if we put on a good movie and I'll make us some dinner after I clean up the house, okay?"

I hope he never comes back. I wish he were dead.

I set the girls up with one of their favorite movies. J.R. was right next to me helping me clean up the mess that David had made. I cried when I saw that the coffee that David had thrown had spilled all over J.R.'s artwork from school.

When J.R. saw the look on my face he said, "Don't worry, I'll draw some more, Mom."

"I'd love that, Sweetie. Thanks."

J.R. said, "Mom, what's really wrong with Daddy? How could he be so mean to us?"

"I told you that your dad was in the hospital because of his drinking too much alcohol. I know it's hard to understand but when he stopped drinking a couple of months ago it became a big adjustment for him to try to live without it. He has to learn how to live day to day all over again. I don't think that he is being mean on purpose. We have to try to help him get better."

"How can we do that?" J.R. asked.

I said, "This is all new to me too. I'm learning how to change some things that will help us all to get through this. As soon as I figure it out, I'll share it with you. But for now, please try not to worry. I will always be here to take care of you and your sisters and to keep you all safe, okay?"

"Okay Mom, I love you," J.R. said as he hugged me tight.

I said, "I love you too. Thanks for your help. I'll get the rest. Go watch TV with your sisters, okay?"

I gave him another hug then and sent him off to the living room.

As I picked up the picture from the hallway floor, I felt angry and afraid. But somehow . . . I still felt hopeful.

It had been only a short time since David had left treatment. He spent thirty days in the hospital. Surely he must remember how difficult it was to get through detox. Some of the therapy that he went through was heart wrenching for him.

He couldn't possibly choose any other path but the one to recovery and a new life, could he? Of course he would choose to be better or all that time would have been wasted. Maybe I just needed to give him more time.

The photo that he'd ripped off the wall was from the day that Valerie was baptized. We all had smiles on our faces. This was the second time that David had thrown this particular picture to the floor. The photo itself was still intact. I thought I could replace the glass . . . again. The gap in the wall was a different story. He had pulled the frame off the wall with such force that it had left a big hole in the wall. It wouldn't be the first time that I'd gotten the Spackle out to make repairs.

Here I had thought that after his being in treatment, I could expect a calm and happy and peaceful kind of life. That was not the case at all.

David raged through the house occasionally while he drank but now that he was sober it seemed to be happening even more frequently. That was probably because he was home more now. He was even harder to tolerate now, than he had been while he was drinking and using cocaine. At least when he was using, he would just come home and pass out most of the time. This was crazy.

Maybe he was right. Maybe this was all my fault. Maybe I should have left things the way they were. Maybe I was responsible for making things even more difficult for all of us.

I got out a bucket with a rag and some soapy water to wash down the kitchen wall and the floor. I moved some of the magnets on the refrigerator to cover the new dent. I found a piece of cardboard large enough to cover the broken glass on the back door. I figured I'd deal with that more tomorrow.

I could feel the rage building inside me. How dare he behave that way in front of the kids! He could speak to me however he felt like. I could take it. He could treat me any way he chose. I could tolerate it.

But not my precious children. Oh no, you are not going to hurt them! I can take the abuse but you are not going to hurt them!

What kind of permanent damage was he creating inside each one of them? They were becoming more and more afraid of him. His conduct was becoming more and more unbearable and unpredictable.

I could only do so much to protect them physically. I couldn't protect them emotionally.

His behavior was killing me . . . slowly.

David came home late that night and just slithered into bed next to me without a word. I pretended to be sleeping like I had so many nights before just to avoid speaking to him.

I was preparing breakfast for the kids the next morning when David walked in dressed for work.

"Did you pack me a lunch?" he asked gruffly.

"It's right there on the counter by your keys," I said.

He grabbed the brown bag and without another word he was out the back door.

No apology. Nothing.

How the hell can you behave like that and not apologize?

There was a collective sigh of relief from all of us left in the kitchen. I didn't dare say anything else to him. I didn't want a repeat of last night. I couldn't talk to him. He was making it impossible.

I have to talk to someone! I have to! Before I go nuts!

I arranged a sitter that day so that I could go to an Al-Anon meeting the very next day, before our next ACG meeting. I would go while he was gone to work for the day.

CHAPTER 10

I T WAS A FRIGID CHICAGO day as I walked into the nearby school where the Al-Anon meeting was held. I felt warm and my palms were sweaty despite the weather. To say that I was nervous was an understatement.

There was an older, white haired woman standing outside the teacher's lounge doorway. She had a big smile on her face as she spoke to a young woman in front of me who looked just as nervous as I was.

"I'm Cathy. Welcome to you. What's your first name?"

She said very quietly, "My name is Carol. This is the first time that I'm here. Am I in the right place? Is this the Al-Anon meeting?"

"Why, yes you are. We are all happy that you are here Carol . . . welcome. Please come on in and grab a cup of coffee," said Cathy.

Carol looked about my same age. Her dark hair was long and curly. She wore jeans and a blue sweater.

Cathy then looked to me and said, "Welcome to you. If you are looking for Al-Anon you are in the right place."

"Hi," I said. "My name is Karen. This is my first meeting as well."

"Happy that you are here. Please come in and make yourself comfortable. The meeting is about to start."

As I walked in, I saw that there was a large circle of mostly empty chairs. There were at least a dozen women who were standing near the coffee table chatting away as if they were at a party.

Am I really in the right place? How could they sound so happy? They couldn't possibly be living like I am!

There was another table that was full of literature. I stood in front of the table right next to Carol and browsed the titles.

I said, "I heard that you are brand new here. So am I. My name is Karen."

As she turned to me she said with a half-smile, "It's nice to meet you, Karen. I'm Carol."

"What could they be laughing about over there?" I said as I turned my head towards the women on the other side of the room.

"I have no idea," said Carol rather sarcastically.

There was a sign on the table before us that said, *HELP YOURSELF TO LITERATURE.* So I did. There was a list of neighborhood meetings and a pamphlet that was titled, *HOW TO FOLLOW THE 12 STEPS OF AL-ANON.* There was also a little booklet that was titled *SPONSORSHIP.*

Carol had such a friendly face that I felt a connection with her immediately. We sat down next to each other as the meeting began.

Cathy seemed to be in charge and as soon as the group of us quieted down she said, "I welcome you all to this meeting." As she looked in the direction of where Carol and I sat, she said, "I especially want to welcome those of you who are new today."

I was relieved when she said nothing else to Carol and me directly because I was not ready to speak.

She read from a notebook, "The Al-Anon Family Groups are a fellowship of relatives and friends of alcoholics who share their experience, strength, and hope in order to solve their common problems. We believe alcoholism is a family illness and that changed attitudes can aid recovery. Al-Anon has but one purpose, to help families of alcoholics. We do this by practicing the twelve steps, by welcoming and giving comfort to families of alcoholics, and by giving understanding and encouragement to the alcoholic."

Cathy went on to say, "Like usual at our meetings, we'd like to go around the circle and introduce ourselves. We like to share our first names only. You can tell us why you are here if you like, whatever you are comfortable with. My name is Cathy. My parents are both alcoholic so I've been dealing with this disease all my life. When I married an alcoholic as well, I figured that I must be doing something wrong. I was led to Al-Anon through a very good friend of mine. I will be forever grateful to her. It has saved my life and kept me sane for the last fifteen years."

The next person to speak sat right next to Cathy. She was a middle aged woman with short blonde hair who wore a long skirt over her large frame. You could tell she was a smoker by the raspiness in her voice.

She spoke very fast and said "Hi every one. My name is Janet. I live with an active alcoholic. He's my husband. We've been married for twenty years. He's been drinking ever since we got married. I didn't realize it was a problem until we were married for about five years. I've been coming to Al-Anon meetings for about ten years now."

Each person around the circle introduced themselves. It was Carol's turn before mine.

Her voice shook a bit as she said, "Hi. My name is Carol. My husband is the alcoholic in my life. This is my first meeting."

And as she looked in my direction, all of the participants who were familiar with the protocol at meetings said together, "Hi Carol."

I said, "Hello. My name is Karen. I've been married to an alcoholic for about six years now. He was in treatment for thirty days and has been home now for several weeks. This is my first meeting."

And again there was a resounding, "Hi Karen."

I was so relieved when they continued around the circle and all eyes were no longer on me. After all had introduced themselves we got to the meat of the meeting.

Cathy said, "We have been working on the steps of the program, one each week. Today we are going to discuss step number four. It reads, *Made a searching and fearless moral inventory of ourselves.* Who would like to start?"

Janet said, "I will. I have worked on this step more than once and I find that when I concentrate on this step, I can take the focus off of my alcoholic and put it back on myself because I know that in reality I'm the only person that I can change. I can change how I react to him which makes me feel better and in turn probably helps him as well. I am truly grateful for my alcoholic because without him, I may never have come to the self-realizations that I have.

Grateful for your alcoholic?? Are you kidding me??

I laughed inside as I raised my eyebrows. I looked at Carol and I could see by the look on her face that she was most probably thinking the very same thing! We gave a knowing smirk to each other as we listened to more.

As a few more people talked about their experiences, I looked at my watch and realized that over an hour had already passed.

Cathy said, "Thanks so much everybody for sharing what you have learned in your own lives about this step. We can move along to step number five next week if you are all agreeable to that."

Most of the regulars there nodded their heads in agreement.

Cathy said, "So think about step number five this week to prepare. It reads, *Admitted to God, to ourselves and to another human being the exact nature of our wrongs.*"

Huh? I wonder what that means!

Cathy went on to say, "There are a couple of things I'd like to share before we close today. I don't think that anyone brought up this topic tonight. I'm bringing it up especially for the benefit of Karen and Carol. Please take a look on your way out at our literature, especially the brochure titled, Sponsorship. Sponsorship gives members an opportunity to get personal support from someone more experienced in the program. These relationships are voluntary. Members ask another member to be their sponsor when they believe that person will be suitable as a mentor in applying the program."

Janet chimed right in and said, "I chose a sponsor right at my first meeting. There was a woman there who seemed to have her act together so much better than me and I just asked her right away. She was so helpful to me in making me feel sane again!"

"One more thing," Cathy said. "If you don't have a copy, I'd like to suggest that you get this book, *ONE DAY AT A TIME IN AL-ANON*. It's like our Bible here. We have it over there on the table with all the other handouts. The price of the book is five dollars."

Carol and I looked at each other again as everyone around the circle joined hands and said together, "God grant me the serenity to accept the things I cannot change, courage to change the things I can, and wisdom to know the difference."

The meeting was over except for the people milling around now talking. I turned to Carol and said, "Have you got one of those books? I'm going to get one for myself."

She said, "I think I'll get one too."

We became fast friends immediately.

As we walked out together, "I said quietly, "Oh my God! That was something else. Can you believe how long Cathy and Janet have been coming here?"

Carol said, "I was thinking the same thing! Do they expect us to come to these meetings for years and years?"

I said, "I know I'm not about to! That's crazy! And how about when Janet said she was grateful for her alcoholic? Is she nuts? How could she be grateful?"

Carol laughed as she said, "How funny that you and I were thinking the same thing at the same time. I am NOT grateful for my alcoholic! That's for sure!"

"Neither am I! Far from it!"

Carol said, "There's a great coffee shop just a couple of blocks from here. Have you got time for a quick cup? We can talk some more."

I said, "That sounds great! I told my babysitter I'd be a couple of hours anyway. I'll just follow you, okay?"

"Great! See you there," said Carol.

As Carol and I drank coffee, our conversation was so easy; I felt like we'd known each other for years. We just clicked.

"What a relief to be talking to someone like you who's going through some of the same crap as me," I said.

"It is a relief. I'm happy to have met you," said Carol

I said, "So how long have you been married?"

"I've been married to my husband Joe for six years. We have a four-year-old son together. His name is Joey too," said Carol.

"How about you, Karen?"

"My husband, David, and I have been married for six years as well but we've known each other since I was thirteen. We were high school sweethearts. We have three kids together . . . two girls and one boy. I think I have a picture in my wallet," I said.

As I showed Carol the picture she said, "Aww, they are so cute!"

"Thanks," I said. "I don't know what I'd do without them. They are the only reason I stay sane."

Carol said, "I know what you mean. My husband doesn't even spend time with my son and me. He sits in the spare bedroom every night just staring at the TV in there while he drinks . . . one beer after another. It's the same thing every night. I really don't know how much longer I can take it."

I asked, "Has he ever tried to stop drinking?"

"He's tried more times than I can count. He promises that he's done with it all, but it never lasts more than a couple of weeks at a time and he's right back to it. How did you get your husband to quit?"

"I really didn't leave him a choice. It was either get help or get out. We had an intervention at my house to convince him to go. I couldn't have done it without my brother-in-law who had been through the same thing as David."

Carol said, "You are lucky that he quit."

I said, "I suppose, but it's been several weeks since he's been home and nothing has really changed except that he's not drinking. His behavior is still just as frightening. He's home more than he was before and it seems even harder to tolerate him. I don't trust him to be alone with the kids. He has no patience. All he does is yell at all of us."

"That's too bad," said Carol. "At least my husband is a quiet drunk. I suppose I have that to be grateful for," she said with a giggle.

I said, "That's why I came to this meeting tonight. I'm just beginning to get the fact that I can't change him. I can't make him do what he's supposed to but I'm hopeful that if I change myself in a good way that maybe he will follow suit. All I know is that I have to do something different because my life is no fun the way that it's going now."

"I hear ya," said Carol.

After a second cup of coffee I looked at my watch and said, "I gotta get home. I have to let the babysitter go."

As we put on our coats, Carol said, "This was great. I hope we can do it again. Why don't we exchange phone numbers and we can talk about when we can meet again."

I said, "Sounds great, Carol. I really enjoyed this. I think it's just what I needed. I have a list of several meetings in the area. I think I will try a different one just to see how they compare."

"That sounds good to me," said Carol. "Let me know which meeting you decide to go to and maybe I can meet you there, okay?"

"I'll call you for sure and let you know," I said.

We walked out of the restaurant together and gave each other a quick hug and then parted ways quickly because it was windy and cold now and just starting to get dark out.

As I drove home that day I started to feel just a glimmer of hope for myself.

CHAPTER 11

I STARTED READING THE PAMPHLETS that I had brought home with me from the Al-Anon meeting the very next morning after David had left for work and the kids were all occupied.

I read the one titled *Sponsorship.* And as I recalled what Cathy had said the night before, I knew right away who I would ask to be my sponsor.

My heart was beating fast and hard as I dialed her number. I thought for sure I'd get her voicemail, and I was all ready with the message that I would leave her.

"Hello," she said with that southern drawl.

"Oh, oh, it's you."

"Uh yes, this is Debbie. May I ask who's calling please?"

I said, "Yes, yes of course. Debbie, this is Karen from the after care group. I'm not sure if you remember me but I got your phone number from the list that was passed out at the last meeting."

"Of course I remember you, Karen! How are you?"

"I'm good. I hope that I'm not bothering you. Is this a good time for you to talk?"

"Yes, I have a few minutes," said Debbie.

I said, "I went to my first Al-Anon meeting yesterday."

Debbie said, "How wonderful for you! How was that? How did it go for you?"

"It went pretty well. There were some nice people there. I made a new friend. We went out for coffee afterwards. I think it's a good start anyway."

Debbie said, "I'm very happy to hear that. Now how can I help you today?"

I said, "I picked up several pieces of literature while I was there, and I've decided that I would like to ask someone to be my sponsor. In fact . . . I was wondering if you would consider being my sponsor."

"You know what? I felt a connection with you the minute I laid eyes on you. I would love to do that for you!" said Debbie.

"Whew! I'm so glad," I said. "I was very nervous to ask you but you really seem to have yourself together and you were the first person I thought of to ask."

"Well thank you for that! I'd be honored to be there for you. I'd love to sit down with you and talk some more. Can we plan that after the next ACG? Right now I have to run to a meeting at work."

"That sounds great, Debbie! Thanks so much."

Debbie said, "Feel free to call me between now and then if you want to talk about anything, all right?"

"I will. Thanks again."

As I hung up I breathed a sigh of relief. I felt so accomplished. Finally, I was doing something for myself to make myself feel better. Finally . . . I was taking steps toward recovery. I was doing something different than I'd done before.

I read through another piece of literature . . . *The Twelve Steps of Al-Anon.*

1. *We admitted we were powerless over alcohol-that our lives had become unmanageable.*
2. *Came to believe that a Power greater than ourselves could restore us to sanity.*
3. *Made a decision to turn our will and our lives over to the care of God as we understood Him.*
4. *Made a searching and fearless moral inventory of ourselves.*
5. *Admitted to God, to ourselves, and to another human being the exact nature of our wrongs.*
6. *Were entirely ready to have God remove all these defects of character.*
7. *Humbly asked him to remove our shortcomings.*
8. *Made a list of all persons we had harmed, and became willing to make amends to them all.*
9. *Made direct amends to such people wherever possible, except when to do so would injure them or others.*
10. *Continued to take personal inventory and when we were wrong promptly admitted it.*
11. *Sought through prayer and meditation to improve our conscious contact with God as we understood Him, praying only for knowledge of His will for us and the power to carry that out.*
12. *Having had a spiritual awakening as a result of these steps, we tried to carry this message to others, and to practice these principles in all our affairs.*

Wow, that's a mouthful!

I went on to read that all the references to God did not refer to any God in particular, only to whatever each person believes to be a power greater than themselves. It seemed overwhelming, but I'd always heard that you can eat a whole elephant if need be . . . just one bite at a time.

I made many more realizations about myself as I began to read my *ONE DAY AT A TIME* book.

I began to see that David had been totally in charge of my feelings and my moods. I found myself to be angry when he was angry, sad when he was sad, and happy when he was happy. I wasn't allowed to have my own feelings, and if I dared to even think them, they were quickly squashed by his. There was just no room for mine. Time and space were filled only with his feelings, his wants and needs.

It wasn't until two days later that David started to speak to me again. He never apologized for his behavior . . . his raging around the house. I didn't bring it up either. I didn't want to make him angry. In fact, the quiet wasn't so bad, not when I compared it to the hostility. I thought that maybe we could talk about it at our next ACG, which was actually that same night.

This was his Modus Operandi. It was this way when he drank and used drugs and it was this way now as well. This was the way he tried to control me. He would scream and yell and rage and then not talk to me at all, not a word. He would completely ignore me. He'd talk to the kids, his friends and family, the neighbors, his work associates. Hell, he'd even talk to the dog. You'd never know to listen to him that there was anything wrong at all. I was the recipient of his wrath . . . always.

He'd talk to everyone but me. It was like I didn't even exist. And it wasn't for lack of trying on my part. Every day I would try to talk to him. Nothing I said would get him to talk.

"David, will you be home tonight for dinner?" I'd ask.

Dead silence.

"Will you be going to J.R.'s parent teacher conference with me tonight?"

Dead silence.

Could you please help me sweep up the elephant in the room?

It didn't matter . . . I could ask him anything and he wouldn't even glance my way.

I was just relieved when those silent spells ended, until the next one anyway.

David actually got home in time for dinner with us for a change. As he walked in the door he sighed and said, "What time is the ACG meeting tonight?"

I was a bit startled by the sound of his voice but pretended this was the norm and said, "It starts at seven o'clock, just like every week. We need to leave as soon as Kim gets here so that we won't be late, okay?"

David said, "Yeah, sure. What's for dinner?"

"I made one of your favorites. I made lasagna," I answered, feeling like a weight had been lifted from my shoulders because he was speaking to me.

I can breathe again.

I felt hopeful that he was still willing to go. It seemed like he felt obligated to attend this ACG with me even though I could tell that he wasn't thrilled about it. He wanted to keep up appearances that he was doing what he was supposed to do in order to recover successfully.

I breathed a sigh of relief as I called the kids, "Time for dinner everyone . . . let's go! Come to the table now."

As everyone sat down, I led them in prayer, "Bless us oh Lord for these thy gifts which we are about to receive from thy bounty through Christ our Lord Amen."

It was adorable the way that Gina, and Val in her high chair, bowed their heads and moved their mouths like they were reciting the prayer with the rest of us. I saw the way they peeked at their dad; uncertain as well about his mood.

Gina dared to say, "Feeling better, Daddy?"

David said, "I'm fine. Don't worry . . . I'm fine."

With that we all sighed collectively and as always the kids followed my lead in behaving as best we could like everything was normal. It was normal in our house anyway.

After dinner, David and I had a few minutes alone to talk and I said, "I called Debbie today."

"Debbie who?" asked David.

"From the ACG. You know . . . Keith's girlfriend?"

David said, "Oh . . . her? What did you call her for?"

I said, "I learned about sponsorship at that Al-Anon meeting that I went to, and I decided to ask Debbie to be my sponsor."

"Really? You think that's necessary?"

I said, "Well, yes . . . I do. I'm not too proud to admit that I need help. I want to feel better and she really has her act together."

David said, "I suppose that's okay. You can do whatever you want but I don't even like her."

Go to hell! I wasn't asking for your approval or your permission!

I said, "It doesn't really matter if you like her or not. I'm the one who will be calling her, not you."

"Sure, whatever. I need to get in the shower now if we are going to get out of here on time," David said.

It started to snow again as we headed to the meeting. I turned on the radio and listened to the music. Now that David's several days of silence had passed I didn't want to say anything that might set him off again. It was like walking on eggshells with him. I had to think about every word I said. I just never knew what might piss him off. So silence was oftentimes the easiest solution.

As we walked into the meeting, everyone was already seated. As we sat down in the last two open chairs, I couldn't help but sense that there was a feeling of doom all around the room.

As Debbie smiled at me from across the room and mouthed *hello,* Keith opened up the meeting by saying, "Some of you may have already heard the bad news. Our friend and fellow patient, Charles, was taken by ambulance to the hospital last night and he passed away this morning from liver damage and other alcohol related complications."

A couple of people around the circle gasped in surprise and then for a moment you could hear a pin drop in the room, as everyone took in this information. I could see a look of shock on David's face next to me.

Wow! You really can die from alcoholism!

Keith said, "Not all of you were actually in treatment with Charles so maybe some of you who knew him better could tell us all a little bit more about him."

Pam's husband Dan spoke up, "I roomed with Charles while I was in the hospital. He was one of four men in our room. He and I talked quite a bit. He was a very laid back kind of guy. He had two grown children . . . a boy and a girl and one grandson as well. His daughter visited while he was in the hospital with me. The grandson even sat in his lap as his daughter pushed him around in his wheelchair. He was in his wheelchair almost all of the time. Charles had told me that his son was not speaking to him because of all the crap he'd tolerated from him and because of the way that he'd treated his mom. Charles had huge regrets about that and was hoping that with his sobriety he could mend those fences but now it's too late, I guess."

Debbie said, "What a shame. What a loss."

Keith said, "I have his ex-wife's address here if any of you would like to send a sympathy card. There's a bulletin board over there, as you leave the room. I'll put it up there for any of you who are interested."

"Thanks, Keith," said Dan.

Keith said, "Let this perhaps be a painful lesson for all of us who are dealing with addictions . . . *there but for the grace of God go I.*"

Everyone else in the room shook their heads in agreement.

"Karen," Debbie said. "Can we start off tonight then with you? I spoke to you on the phone the other day. You said that you had gone to your first Al-Anon meeting. Can you tell us? How did that go for you? What was that like?"

I said, "It was good. I was nervous but the people there were nice. I got some really great literature to read, and I actually ended up going out for coffee with a woman I met there. It was really great to talk to someone, one on one, who is dealing with the same things as me."

Debbie said, "Thanks for sharing that, Karen. It's especially helpful to those around the circle here tonight who maybe haven't had a chance to get to a meeting yet. Can you tell us what the best thing was, about the meeting?"

I said, "Yes. You know . . . for so long, I thought I was alone in all of this and I can hardly express what a relief it is to know now that, that's just not true at all. I'm realizing more and more that there are so many people in the same situation as me."

"That's excellent, Karen, thanks," said Debbie. "How about you David? How did you feel about Karen going to Al-Anon?"

David said, "She can do whatever she wants to do. I'm fine with that."

Debbie said, "How did your week go David? You had mentioned at the last meeting that you were a business owner. How's everything going there?"

David said, "My gas station has suffered, of course, because I was gone for a month so it's going to take a little time to get it all back in order but I'm working on it."

Keith said, "What about meetings? How many have you been able to attend since last week?"

"I've gone to two since last week," David said.

Oh my God! You are such a liar! Who do you think you're fooling?

"Have you found them helpful?" asked Keith.

"Yeah, they've been okay."

Is my face red? I'm so embarrassed by you! Even now you can't be honest?

Keith said, "How's your health David? I have to say that you are not looking well."

I could see from the look on David's face that he was getting angry. He shook his head and said, "What do you mean?"

"Your face looks a bit swollen and red and you seem nervous there."

David said, "I'm fine really."

Keith looked right at me and said, "Is that true, Karen? Are there any health issues going on with David?"

I wasn't about to lie. I took a deep breath and I said, "David was diagnosed with diabetes while he was in treatment and he really hasn't addressed it since he got home from the hospital. He seems to think that it will go away magically."

"Is that true, David?" asked Keith.

David said, "They told me that it may have been brought on by my addictions and that my blood sugar may regulate itself given some time."

I knew that I'd probably pay for my boldness but I said, "You are supposed to be going to the doctor to check it closely and you haven't done that yet."

David just looked at me and said, "I have been so busy with the business for the last couple of weeks that I just haven't had time!"

Keith interjected and said, "I hope that the death of Charles will perhaps open your eyes to your own health issues and that you will do what you need to do to take care of your diabetes. I will ask you about it again at the next meeting, okay?"

"Sure," David said.

Debbie said, "Let's move around the circle now and check in with Pam and Dan. How are you two doing tonight?"

As all eyes focused then on this couple, I could feel David's eyes boring a hole into the side of my head but I refused to look at him. I could only hope that he would cool off before the ride home.

I was sick and tired of lying for him to everybody. I couldn't do it anymore. I just couldn't tolerate it for another minute.

You can lie if you want to but I'm not going to do it anymore!

After Pam and Dan spoke for a bit, Keith said. "Thanks to both of you for sharing. Jeff, how are you doing over there?"

When I turned to look in his direction I couldn't help but notice that Jeff's wife, Marie, was already tearing up. She had a crumpled tissue in her hand.

Jeff said, "I'm not good. I was dreading coming here tonight knowing that I would have to admit to relapsing. I told Marie that I had to stay late at work two nights ago when in fact I went with a couple of my friends to the bar and I had a couple of drinks."

Keith said, "How many drinks is a couple Jeff?"

"I had six beers," said Jeff.

"I'm sorry to hear that, but at least you are admitting to it," said Keith.

Jeff said, "Yeah, but that doesn't make me feel any better about it."

Keith asked, "Have you had anything to drink since then?"

"No, I haven't," said Jeff.

Debbie looked at Marie then, who by now had tears running down her cheeks. "Marie, tell us how you are feeling right now."

Marie said, "Of course I feel like crap about it but at least he didn't try to hide it from me. He came home right after, and told me that he'd been drinking again. He cried as he apologized to me over and over."

Keith said, "I have a feeling, Jeff, that no one feels worse about your relapse than you do."

Jeff said, "I feel terrible about it but I called my sponsor the next morning and I went to a meeting with him. I have to stay on track now."

"Why do you think it happened?" asked Keith.

Jeff said, "I got out of the hospital four weeks ago and I had been attending an AA meeting at least every other day. This last week I didn't. So I have no one to blame but myself."

Keith said, "So what are you going to do to make sure this doesn't happen again?"

As Jeff looked at his wife he said, "First I want to apologize to you, Marie, in front of everyone here. I'm so sorry that I made you worry again. I promise I will do what it takes to stay sober for you and for myself. I know what I have to do. I need to be at a meeting every day until I get a firm hold on my sobriety."

Keith said, "We will be checking in on you next week Jeff. I think that for all of us here it's helpful to commit to what we are going to do, out loud to one another. I know that it helps me to follow through with the things that I need to do, to stay sober. I think that if it works for me it will work for some of you here as well."

With that we are going to close this meeting," said Keith. "We will see all of you back here next week at the same time then. Let's end with the Serenity Prayer."

As everyone got up out of their chairs, David said to me, "I'm going to talk to that new guy over there. It's his first night here but I met him in the hospital."

I said, "Sure, that's fine. I want to talk to Debbie anyway."

As I walked up to Debbie, she welcomed me with a big hug and a smile and said, "Let's grab a cup of coffee, Karen, and go sit down and chat."

"That sounds great," I said.

As I sat down with Debbie, I could see that David had walked out into the vestibule where smoking was allowed, with the new guy. He had introduced himself as Andy.

Good, he's occupied. I can talk.

Debbie said, "I'm so excited to be your sponsor, Karen. I want to thank you for trusting me enough to ask me."

"And I want to thank you for agreeing to help me out this way," I said. "Because honestly . . . I'm a wreck. I may not look like it on the outside but sometimes I feel like I'm falling apart."

"Aww . . . Karen, it's okay to feel like that and even more important that you are able to share that with me. Keeping those feelings inside can just make you sick, physically and emotionally."

I shook my head and said, "I know."

Debbie said, "I have been where you are . . . so I know just how you are feeling and I can guarantee you that you will feel better if you continue to make changes, even if they are very small changes."

I said, "I'm willing to do whatever it takes to feel better."

Debbie said, "Wonderful!"

I asked, "So what are you able to help me with as my sponsor? This is all so new to me."

"First of all, I want to give you my work phone number here. I know you have my cell. You can call me at any time, day or night. If I can't talk, I'll just say so. I'll get back to you as soon as I can."

Debbie actually worked right in the building where our meeting was held. She answered phones, coordinated schedules, and did all their paperwork.

"I hope that you are ready because I'm going to be calling you a lot," I said as I laughed. "I don't know what I'm doing. I'm feeling overwhelmed with all the bits of advice I'm getting from here and from Al-Anon and from what I've been reading. I don't know where to start!"

"You've already started, Karen," said Debbie. "You're here. You're going to Al-Anon meetings. You're reading. That's all part of recovering. You want to learn as much as you can about the disease of addiction, and it's just as important to learn about co-dependency. Because like it or not, you are a co-dependent."

"I have to get used to that idea because for so long I thought that this whole thing was entirely his fault. I'm just beginning to realize that maybe there are some things that I've done to make our situation even worse," I said.

Debbie laughed and said, "If you are anything like me that's probably true. I've been guilty myself of making some pretty poor choices along the way but I take comfort in the fact that I am actively doing what it takes now to make some big changes in how I react . . . not only to my alcoholic but to everyone around me."

I said, "I hear you."

Debbie said, "I have found it to be very beneficial for me to put the focus back on myself. I've stopped taking Keith's inventory, and I've started to take my own instead. I want to be the best that I can be and by working on that, I can be the best friend, and daughter, and girlfriend, and employee possible."

"So how do I begin to do all that?" I asked.

"You can start with some small things. When you are uncertain of how to handle any given situation, give me a call and maybe I can help talk you through it to a good resolution. If you are in the middle of a heated moment and you can't make a decision of what to do . . . do nothing until you have some time to think it through," said Debbie.

"Okay, so you are saying that sometimes the best decision is no decision?"

"Exactly," said Debbie.

I replied, "Thanks Debbie. It's always great talking with you."

Debbie said, "Remember you can call me anytime you need to, and remember to take all of this . . . one day at a time."

As we stood up, Debbie grabbed me and gave me an enthusiastic hug and whispered in my ear, "You are going to be fine Karen, no doubt."

"Thanks Debbie. I will talk to you soon," I said.

"I look forward to it," said Debbie.

"Bye bye," I said.

Debbie said, "See you both next week!"

I walked out into the vestibule where David was talking to Andy and another man from another group that I didn't recognize. As I approached them, I could hear the conversation going on.

Andy laughed as he said, "Yes, I have my degree in psychology. Do you think that would have helped me through all this? Apparently not! College was just a good excuse for me to drink!"

David said, "I hear ya! When I was away at college, that's when my drinking got entirely out of control too! Have to admit though . . . it was fun while it lasted! California is beautiful! And it has lots of great bars!"

What? College? What are you talking about? You didn't go to college at all . . .

They were all laughing as I walked up. David said, "Karen, this is Derrick. Derrick, this is my wife, Karen. Derrick is in another ACG here. I met him at one of my AA meetings."

I said, "Nice to meet you, Derrick."

139

"Nice to meet you," said Derrick as he offered his hand to me.

California? What the hell are you talking about?

David said, "Hey, we'll see you guys next week. Let's go, Karen."

As we walked through the parking lot to the car, I could see that another couple of inches of snow had fallen. It was the kind of fresh, light undisturbed snow that looked like glitter on the ground. It was beautiful.

When we got into the car, David asked me "Would you mind calling the doctor for me while I am at work tomorrow to make me an appointment? I need to get my blood sugar checked."

Wow, you actually listened?

I said, "I can do that, yes. What made you decide that?"

David said, "I'll admit it. The news of Charle's death has scared the crap out of me!"

"It's awful for sure. I really feel bad for his family," I said.

David said, "He was a nice guy. I feel bad too. What a waste."

"That could be you David. I'm so glad that you have stopped drinking and using drugs."

"I know," said David quietly.

"We have a real chance here to come together and be a healthy family. I'm willing to work on this with you if you can promise me the same," I said.

And for just a moment, blessedly so, I could feel his gratitude when he said, "I want to work on this too. I was really far gone there with the cocaine. I could have died, I know. You saved my life, Karen. Thanks for forcing me into treatment."

A tear ran down my cheek as I looked out at the falling snow. I took a deep breath to coax the lump out of my throat so that I wouldn't cry when I said, "You can thank me by being well. Do what you need to do to be healthy. Don't do it for me either. Do it for you," I said.

David said, "I will. I promise. I will."

I said, "I have to ask you something."

"What?"

I replied, "What were you talking about in there? You never went to college and you've never been to California . . . have you?"

"No."

I shook my head in confusion and said, "Well, why did you tell them that?"

"Oh, I don't know. It's no big deal."

"I find it strange, David. Why would you lie about that? Do you think that they won't like you if you are honest about who you are? Can't you just be yourself?"

He replied, "I said it's no big deal!"

This wasn't the first time that I'd heard David lying to people in casual conversation for no apparent reason. It baffled me really . . .

I don't get it. I don't understand you.

A few minutes passed by as we were both lost in our own thoughts.

David became more talkative then and said, "Andy and I were talking about all the meetings that he goes to. A couple of them are not too far from our house, so I told him that I'm going to attend a couple of them with him."

"That would be great for you David," I said.

You're not yelling at me. I'm shocked.

"Now that might mean that I won't be able to sit down with you and the kids for dinner. The meetings he told me about are right around dinnertime," said David.

I said, "I think that right now meetings are important for you. That has to be your first priority," I said.

Holy Crap! I called him out on his lying and he's not yelling at me.

David said, "Andy told me that a few of the patients that I met in the hospital who are in a different ACG attend these meetings too, so I'll know some of the people. It will be good to see them."

"That sounds really good for you David," I said.

Why isn't he yelling at me?

David said, "He also told me that he and some of the others go get coffee and socialize after the meetings. You wouldn't mind that, would you?"

"I wouldn't mind that at all. That would be fine. Whatever you have to do to stay sober is fine with me," I said.

I don't care why he isn't yelling at me! I'm just glad that he isn't!

He never even mentioned the fact that I had called him out at the meeting. The death of a fellow patient had obviously impacted David in a good way. His talking to Andy had obviously helped his mood as well. I could only hope that David would follow through with his promises moving forward.

I realized now too, that perhaps I could use the ACG as a safe place for me to say to David the things that I was too afraid to say out loud to him at home, for fear of his reaction.

For the first time in a long time, and like the undisturbed snow on the sides of the road that night, hope was in the air for us. I felt like this could be a fresh new start for us both together and apart.

Chapter 12

I BEGAN TO FEEL LIKE I could think just a bit more clearly with every Al-Anon meeting that I attended. I tried several different locations before I found my favorite one. At many meetings, I didn't even need to speak. I just sat back and listened to everyone else. Their stories gave me a wealth of information. I was able to take what I liked with me and leave the rest.

David actually seemed to be making an effort to get to his meetings as well. He attended rather sporadically though. One week, he would go two or three times and the next week he would skip altogether. I wondered sometimes if he was only going so that he could report to Keith and Debbie at our ACG that he in fact was attending.

There were good days at home and bad days with David. The bad seemed to outweigh the good, and unfortunately I couldn't seem to remove myself emotionally from his moods. But at least I began to realize the things about myself that I needed to change. His mood was my mood for so long that these habits were incredibly difficult to change. I didn't even know what my alternatives were . . . these habits were so ingrained in me. But little by little, I was able to make small changes.

I was in the kitchen cooking dinner when the back door opened and slammed shut hard. It was David.

He threw his keys on the kitchen counter next to me, gave me a dirty look, and went right into our bedroom without a word to me or the kids. I could hear that he had turned the TV on rather loudly.

My immediate impulse was to drop what I was doing and run right in there and ask him what was wrong and try to make it better for him. That's what I'd always done before. This time I did something different.

I grabbed my cordless phone and went downstairs to the laundry room where the dryer was running so that I wouldn't be heard. I dialed Debbie's number and was relieved when she answered the phone with her friendly, "Hello."

I said, "Hi Debbie, this is Karen."

"How you doin', Karen?"

"Not great. I need your help," I said. "David just walked in the house in a terrible mood and I'm tempted to try to make it better like I always have. What should I do?"

"Well," Debbie said, "what's going on right now with you and the kids?"

I said, "The kids are watching cartoons. I was just getting dinner ready when he walked in."

"And where is David right now?" asked Debbie.

"He's in our bedroom with the TV blaring. He's probably just waiting for me to come in there to ask him what's wrong."

Debbie said, "What if you do something different this time? You just take care of those kids and yourself and get dinner on the table. You can invite David to join you. You can pretend that you didn't even notice his bad mood. Don't ask him what's wrong. For a change, see if he can bring it up himself."

"Okay, I'll try that. Thanks Debbie. I'll let you know what happens."

As I went back into the kitchen, I said to J.R., "Please come and help me set the table for dinner, Honey."

"Okay, Mom. What's wrong with Daddy? He didn't say anything when he walked past me."

I said, "I don't know. Maybe he will tell us. No worries."

I could see the nervous look on his face as I gave him a quick hug and said, "After you set the table, please tell the girls to wash their hands for dinner, okay?"

"Okay, Mom."

I certainly couldn't blame him for being nervous. So many times before, David's tirades began with him coming in the back door and slamming it behind him. So many of his fits of rage started out with him hiding in our bedroom. This time though, I was going to do something different. I hoped that my reaction to him would make his behavior different this time.

I hoped too that if I reacted differently to David that in turn I could put the kids at ease as well. Kids are so smart. They absorb so much more than we realize.

The meatloaf smelled wonderful, and after I poured the gravy into a bowl and set it on the table, I collected the girls from the bathroom after helping them dry their hands.

As the kids got seated around the table, I knocked on the bedroom door where David was and as I opened the door I looked directly at him said, "Dinner is ready. Come join us."

"I'll be right there," said David.

As I walked back into the kitchen, I heard the kids giggling. It was adorable. J.R. had helped Valerie into her highchair and he was tickling her. She was laughing hard which was making Gina laugh even harder.

Thank you God for these kids! What would I do without them?

I laughed out loud and said, "Okay now, J.R., thanks for your help but please sit down now so we can eat."

"Okay, Mom," said J.R.

David walked into the kitchen then and sat down. He looked totally worn out and tired. But at least he sat down with us.

Gina said, "Mmmmm, this is yummy, Mommy."

I said, "I'm glad that you like it, Sweetie."

As I put a slice of meatloaf onto Valerie's tray I asked, "J.R., what was the best part of your day today?"

"That's easy!" J.R. said enthusiastically. "Mrs. Merlo had to leave the room for a while and she left an eighth grader in charge and we got to play games!"

I said, "That sounds fun."

J.R. said, "The best part was when she came back, she gave us all candy!"

"Sweet," I said.

Gina said, "I want candy!"

"Me too!" said Valerie.

I laughed and I said, "Later kids, let's finish our dinner now."

J.R. said, "What was the best part of your day, Dad?"

"No part," he grumbled. "Hmmm . . . maybe this dinner."

"Daddy, you're being silly," said Gina.

David smiled then as he replied, "Yes, I am."

I didn't ask David anything. I was just going to wait and see if he would talk to me and let me know what was bothering him for a change, instead of me trying to pry it out of him.

David lingered at the table after the kids were excused.

I was cleaning up the table and loading the dishwasher when he said, "Things are not going well at the station at all. I'm not sure what's going to happen. There just isn't enough fucking money to cover all the fucking expenses."

I sat down next to him and said, "Is there anything that I can do to help?"

He shook his head slowly and said, "I wish there was . . . but I just don't know if I'll be able to pull it out." He choked up as he said, "I'm afraid I could lose the business entirely."

I stood up and leaned over to hug him.

"I'm so sorry, David. I don't know what to say."

"There's still a chance that I can work it out somehow, but it's not looking good. I have a meeting tomorrow with the higher ups from the gas company. I'll know more then."

I sat down again and said, "It's probably even more important that you go to your AA meeting tonight with Andy, yes?"

David said, "I already called him to cancel. I can't even think about that tonight."

"Did he think it was a good idea for you to skip?"

"I don't really give a fuck what he thought! I'm not going tonight!"

I said, "Fine, whatever."

I was not about to rile him up now, any more than he already was.

He pushed the chair back behind him and got up without another word and went back to our bedroom and shut the door.

After cleaning up the kitchen, I gave the kids their baths and after tucking them all in for the night, I dared to open the door to my bedroom. David was dozing . . . having fallen asleep on the bed with half his clothes on. I didn't dare disturb him.

I tiptoed out of the room and went back to the laundry room and dialed Debbie's number.

I said, "Hi Debbie, it's me again. Can you talk for a few minutes?"

"Yes, I can," she said. "How's everything going?"

I said, "Actually, not too bad. I did what you suggested and David came to the table for dinner, and there was no yelling at all."

Debbie said, "I'm so glad to hear that, Karen. Did he tell you what was on his mind?"

"I couldn't believe it . . . he actually did tell me!"

"Do you want to talk about what it was that was bothering him?"

I said, "Yes. He is really struggling at his gas station. Apparently the financial situation there is not good at all. There's just not enough money to go around to pay for everything."

Debbie said, "I'm sorry to hear that but this situation is totally out of your control, Karen. All you can do is be supportive to him no matter what happens."

I said, "I'm trying to do that. He's so sad. It hurts to see him that way. It's breaking my heart. That business is his pride and joy."

"I hear you," said Debbie. "I'm so proud of you for reacting in a different way tonight than usual. It sounds like it kept peace in your house anyway."

"It did," I said. "I'm amazed really that for this time anyway . . . the result was different than what normally may have escalated into a bad situation for all of us here. Thanks so much for your help, Debbie!"

Debbie said, "I didn't do anything really, Karen. You are doing all the work."

I said, "I guess you are right there."

Debbie said, "So what did David do then to help himself? Did he call his sponsor? Did he go to a meeting?"

"This morning when he left for work, he told me that he planned on going to a meeting with Andy tonight but after we spoke at dinner he said he wasn't up to going. I tried to talk him into it but he started to get aggravated so I dropped the subject," I said.

Debbie said, "I'm glad that you did, Karen, because he knows what he is supposed to be doing. You don't need to tell him. You can't make him do anything. You just have to focus on yourself and what you are doing to get well."

"You're right," I said. "I just wanted to let you know that we are okay here for today. I'll talk to you soon."

"Bye bye, Karen," said Debbie.

"Bye bye."

I often felt overwhelmed at home. I felt like I was raising the kids by myself. When David had been drinking he never really had anything to do with the discipline and care of the children. How could he? He was never home.

Now that he was home more often, he tried to discipline.

J.R. and Gina were watching TV one night. J.R. grabbed an M&M right out of a little pile in front of Gina.

Gina screamed, "GIVE THAT BACK TO ME!"

J.R. said, "Nope," as he popped it into his mouth.

David yelled, "Go to your room, J.R! Right now!"

As J.R. went to his room, I said to David, "Are you kidding? You think that's reasonable?"

"Yeah, I do!"

I said, "Well, I don't! It's an M&M! There's a much simpler way to handle that. He doesn't need to go to his room."

David got up and then and said, "Go to hell!"

I just shook my head as David went to hide in his room.

You don't know what the hell you are doing. Good riddance!

I went right to J.R.'s room and told him to come back and join me and the girls.

David's discipline was always over the top. It was excessive to say the least and I wasn't about to let him screw up what I'd worked so hard to do in giving the kids guidelines in their behavior. He'd only confuse them. He didn't have a clue as to how I was handling things.

It was very difficult for me to even consider allowing David to be a part of their discipline. So after several failed attempts at parenting in a constructive manner, he pretty much gave up. That was fine with me. Kids need consistency. I didn't mind being the disciplinarian.

Chapter 13

WE WERE ABOUT HALF WAY through the six months of ACG meetings that were offered to us when the topic for the evening was "Alcoholism, the Disease."

Keith said, "They say that when you start drinking and doing drugs, for those of us who become addicted, that our emotional development is arrested. So when we stop, we are essentially at the emotional age we were when we started. I started getting high when I was eighteen and I got clean at age thirty five. So three years ago at age thirty five, my emotions were that of an eighteen year old. A pretty scary thought, yeah?"

You could hear a few giggles in the room.

Wow! That explains a lot!

David had been drinking since he was fifteen!

Dan said, "Holy shit! I never heard that before."

Keith said, "Yes, I'm afraid that it's true. I know for me when I learned this . . . it helped me to understand why it's suggested to us as addicts that we stay on track by going to lots of meetings. We have to basically learn how to live all over again! We have to grow up and quick!"

Jeff said, "Why does that happen?"

Keith said, "It's because the use of alcohol prevented us from experiencing and working through the usual developmental stages associated with emerging adulthood. That's why a lot of us tend to be impulsive, angry individuals with a low frustration tolerance and poor long range planning abilities."

Debbie said, "Wow, that's interesting!"

"It is," said Keith, "but I'm the first to admit it. Those things are true about me. I was pretty hard headed when I first realized this because I didn't want to admit that I had these shortcomings."

"How did you start to overcome all of that?" asked Jeff.

"I got myself a sponsor early on . . . someone who had lots of years in the program and then I listened to him and did what I was told," said Keith with a laugh.

I could see that David was listening to Keith. He was always happiest at this meeting when someone else was doing the talking. It meant that there was no one bothering him. There was no one asking him important questions.

Debbie said, "Geez, I'm glad that I didn't know you then. I don't know if I would have liked you at all if you were acting like you were eighteen!"

Everyone around the circle laughed.

Keith said, "I cannot emphasize enough how important it is, if you as addicts choose to be healthy, that you be honest with yourselves. It's an imperative part of any successful recovery."

"I was just talking to my sponsor about that today," said Dan. "I know that my ability to con myself and others around me is superlative! I know how to manipulate people into thinking what I want them to think. I'm just now beginning to realize that it's not a good thing."

His wife Pam said, "I can attest to that! You are full of shit!"

Dan began to laugh with his wife and everyone in the room joined in. The laughter lightened the atmosphere in the room for a moment until we moved onto the next topic.

Debbie said, "David, you're quiet tonight. How are things going at your business? We haven't talked about that in a couple of weeks."

David said, "Things are not going well. In fact it's pretty shitty. There are a lot of financial problems I'm dealing with and I'm just not sure how the hell it will all turn out."

Debbie said, "I'm sorry to hear that. Do you think that the situation you are in now has anything to do with your addictions?"

"No, not really. There have been issues there for a long time. Business in general has just been slow."

Talk about Denial! Are you serious?

Keith said, "Can you elaborate, David? What are some of the issues there?"

David said, "A few months back I put a lot of money up to buy out my partner. We were not getting along at all, and it got to the point where one of us had to go. I took over the business myself, and now I'm playing catch up financially."

Keith asked, "Do you think that your addictions had anything to do with your not being able to get along with your partner?"

David said, "No, I don't think so."

Keith smiled as he said, "Seriously? Are you kidding? How could it not have affected your partnership?"

Wow! Someone is finally calling you out!

"It just didn't," said David.

"So you used cocaine every day, and you don't think it affected your relationship with your partner who you worked with every day?" asked Keith.

David said, "Nope," as he shook his head.

Keith said, "I don't know who you think you are kidding. It had to affect your work relationship. Cocaine is damn expensive. How did you pay for it?"

I could see David's face redden as he squirmed in his seat.

He was getting pissed but Keith asked again, "How could you have possibly supported your habit by any other means than by taking money from your business?"

Holy Shit!

David said, "I started selling it out of the gas station!"

Keith asked, "How did that work for you?"

"Not well," said David. "It would have worked just fine if I only sold it. My problem was using. It only took my using one time, for me to want to do it over and over again. I was hooked just like that."

All eyes were on David. Everyone was listening so closely. I thought that surely everyone there that night must have heard my heart pounding, for it was pounding so hard.

Keith had a way of getting to the heart of the matter. He didn't care if anyone he confronted in group got mad at him.

He said, "Thanks for owning up to that, David. Honesty is the only thing that will get you through this recovery and only if you want it bad enough."

"Yeah," said David. "I know."

Keith said, "So tell us what specifically you are dealing with this week."

David said, "A couple of days ago, the big boss was in and he pretty much threatened that if I can't come up with the money that the gas provider is owed within a week, they are going to shut me down."

Keith asked, "How did you handle that, David?"

"I told him that I would do what I could to come up with the money," said David.

"What I really mean is, for the sake of your recovery, how did you handle that?" asked Keith.

David said, "I went to a meeting that evening."

No! You didn't! You hid in your bedroom!!!!!!

The second he said that Debbie looked over at me. I could tell from the look in her eye she remembered, without doubt, that he had done no such thing. That was the night that I had called her for help in dealing with his mood. She knew he was lying but she didn't say anything out loud.

Keith asked, "Was that helpful to you, David?"

David said, "Yeah, a little I guess."

Keith said, "Well, we all hope that you are able to work this out David, but I'm sure that you realize that all this bullshit you are dealing with is an absolute consequence of some of the poor choices that you have made because of your addictions."

"I know," said David.

"Do you really?" Keith asked. "Because sometimes I listen to you and I think that you are only saying what you think I want to hear."

David looked surprised. He said, "I get that I've made some bad choices . . . but the gas station has had problems for a while now. That's all I'm saying."

Keith said, "Okay, let's move along now to some more information about the disease of addiction."

I sat back in my chair as I tried to listen to the facts that Keith shared with the group. I didn't dare to even look in David's direction. I was sure that he was ready to run out of the room. I already felt so embarrassed about his lying I could hardly breathe. I wanted to get through this meeting and get out to the car and go home. I had a nervous feeling in the pit of my stomach as I thought about what I might be in for on the ride home with David.

As the meeting came to a close David said, "Let's go. I'm not hanging around to socialize with anyone tonight."

I said, "Okay, let me just say good bye to Debbie."

"Make it quick," David said.

At that moment, Keith walked right up to both of us with a smile on his face. He reached out for David's hand and shook it and said, "Don't mean to piss you off David. I'm just trying to be of some help in making you realize the truth of your life now. I've been where you are. I know how you feel. This shit is not easy."

David said, "I hear you, Man."

Keith said, "We'll see you both next week."

As Keith walked away David said, "I'll go outside and warm up the car."

"Okay," I said.

As I walked up to Debbie then, she had her arms outstretched to give me a much needed hug. As I accepted it gratefully she said, "That was a rough one for both of you, wasn't it?"

"Yes, it was."

Debbie said, "This whole process is difficult for all of us . . . no doubt. You will be fine though. You are doing great through all of this, Karen."

"It doesn't feel like it sometimes," I said.

"I know just how you feel. I was where you are a couple of years ago. I promise it will get better."

I said, "Thanks Debbie, but I have to go now. He's anxious to leave. I will call you tomorrow, okay?"

"That sounds great! You two be careful driving," Debbie said with a smile.

I slid into the car seat next to David. He had the radio on loud as if to drown out any chance of a conversation. I was fine with that. I was as happy as he was to be on our way home.

I breathed a sigh of relief as I watched the snow falling gently around us.

CHAPTER 14

THE PHONE RANG JUST AS I was tiptoeing out of the girl's room. I had read their favorite book to them as they nodded off for their afternoon nap.

I sat down on my bed with a sigh as I picked up the cordless phone.

I could hardly hear David as he said quietly, "They are here emptying the underground tanks. It's over."

"Oh my God! What? Are you kidding? How did that happen so fast?"

I could hear him choking up as he said, "I don't know. The truck just showed up a few minutes ago. The driver didn't even say anything to me. He just shoved the hoses into the ground openings and started syphoning the gas out of the tanks."

I started to cry as I said, "I'm so sorry, David. I wish there was something that I could do to help."

David said, "There's nothing any of us can do. It's over. I've lost the fucking business."

"I don't even know what to say."

"There's nothing," David said.

I could hear that he was crying. His heart was breaking, and mine was breaking right alongside his.

I said, "I love you, David. We will get through this somehow."

David said despondently. "I don't know how. I just wanted to call you and tell you what was happening. I don't know what happens next. I don't know when I'll be home. I just don't know."

With that the line went dead.

I just sat there stunned for a moment. Our livelihood was gone. Just like that it was gone. Three kids to house and to feed and no job between the two of us.

Holy Crap, what are we gonna do?

The tears were streaming down my face as I picked up the phone again and called Debbie. Thank God she picked up the phone on the first ring.

"Hello," she said.

"Debbie . . . this is Karen," I said through my tears.

"Karen, what's wrong? Are you okay?"

I said, "David just called. What we hoped would never happen just did. They are right now removing the gas from the underground tanks at his gas station. Without gas, there is no business."

Debbie said, "Oh my gosh, Karen, I am so sorry to hear that. Are you okay?"

"No, not really," I said through my tears. "I don't know what we are going to do. While he was in treatment, I promised him that I would do my best to keep his business going and look what's happened!"

Debbie said, "Don't you dare go there! This is not your fault! You did do the best that you could for him but his business was definitely in trouble already before you ever stepped foot in there. This is his responsibility! Not yours!"

"I guess that's probably true," I said.

"There is no doubt about it, Karen," said Debbie "This is totally his doing. Now I feel really bad for him and for you but you are not at fault in any way for this."

"I feel so bad. My heart is breaking for him. He was such a proud business owner. It was his life. I just don't know what to do to help him," I said.

Debbie said, "Listen to me, Karen. There is nothing you can do to help him out of this situation. In fact, he has to experience this loss. He needs to face the consequences for his actions. You cannot repair it or protect him from it. You would not be helping him if you took that away from him."

"Maybe you're right," I said.

Debbie said, "There are no maybes about it! I am right this time. No doubt! All you can do is be there for him . . . but you can't fix this. It is what it is."

I wiped my face and said with a sigh, "You're right. Life will go on. We will figure this out."

"Yes you will," Debbie said. "Sometimes an addict has to experience great loss in order to realize that they are helpless from this disease and all the hardships that go along with it."

I said, "Well, this is about as big a loss as I can imagine for him, so I guess all I can hope is that this is the worst consequence we will have to face."

Debbie said, "He has you, Karen, and the kids. This is certainly not his biggest loss! It's just a business. He's capable of working somewhere else, isn't he?"

"Yes, I guess so," I said.

Debbie said, "Now just as importantly, you need to take care of yourself, Karen. You did that by calling me for encouragement. What else can you do to help yourself through this emotionally?"

"I was planning on going to an Al-Anon meeting tomorrow afternoon, but with what just happened I'm not sure if I'll be able to make it."

Debbie said, "Karen, it's even more important now that you go. Don't let David's stuff get in the way of your recovery. He has to deal with his crap and you have to deal with yours."

"I guess you are right. I will go for sure," I said.

Debbie said, "I have a meeting to get to now, but please call me later if you need to. I'm always here for you."

"Thanks Debbie. I don't know what I'd do without you," I said.

"I'm happy that I can help you, Karen. I have a sponsor too, who has been with me since the beginning of my recovery. I feel the same way about her as you do about me. I think that you are doing great!"

I said, "Thanks Debbie, I'll talk to you later."

As I hung up, I thought about the day's events so far. I was just beginning to realize what a focused kind of concentration it was going to take to handle all the obstacles in my life in a new and healthier way. I knew that for now, I really needed Debbie's input to get through each challenging day. Her advice and support were becoming invaluable to me quickly. If it meant that I would have to call her five times a day, then I would call her five times a day. The most important thing that I was realizing as of late, was that I was feeling just a bit more empowered and in control of my life.

There's no question that I was afraid though, of what the future would hold for David, and me, and the kids. My mind wandered around all the awful possibilities.

How the hell are we going to make the next house payment? How are we going to pay the utilities? How am I going to feed the kids?

I noticed my *ONE DAY AT A TIME IN AL-ANON* book on the bedside table. I picked it up and looked in the index in the back of the book. I looked up readings about fear. I read that, *We who live with addicts very often wonder, what if . . . and in the process can make ourselves sick with worry and dread about things that haven't even happened yet; things that in fact may never happen. In the end we have wasted so much time feeling anxious over nothing at all when that time could have been spent so much better on something productive. I cannot do anything about things that haven't happened.*

Before I knew it, an hour had gone by, and I could hear the girls begin to stir from their nap. I had just enough time to change them both and to get Val a bottle before we were out the door to pick J.R. up from school.

We all stopped back home for a snack and a quick change for J.R. into his Tae Kwon Do clothes. We were out the door again and into the car for the ride to the school where his class was held.

I smiled all the while as I watched him kick boxing his energy out. I felt like crying, but I had to be strong for the kids. I couldn't lose it.

J.R. looked at me to make sure I was watching as his instructor held a board just below his waist level with one hand on top and the other on the bottom, as J.R. yelled out and with a bare foot kicked that board right in half. All the parents clapped loudly.

Thank you God for the wonderful distractions that are my children!

All the while in the back of my mind were thoughts of David and the despair he must be feeling at the loss of his business. These kids and all the busy work it took to care for them . . . they were my saving grace.

All of the kids were in bed for the night. It was late when I heard the back door open. I'd been watching TV and was just about to doze off when he walked into the room where I was.

My heart sank when I saw him. David's eyes were red from tears as I got up from the couch. His shoulders were sagging in defeat.

"I'm so sorry this has happened, David. I wish there was something that I could do to fix it," I said quietly.

There was such a look of despair on his face as he ran his fingers through his disheveled hair and said, "I feel like my life is over."

As we embraced I said, "Your life is not over. You have me and the kids. We will get through this somehow. I love you."

His shoulders shook with emotion then as he hugged me tighter and said, "I'm so sorry, Karen. I've really fucked up. This is all my fault."

"What's done is done, David," I said. "There is no going back. You can't change what's happened. All we can do now is to move forward."

David collapsed onto the couch then and said, "What the fuck are we going to do?"

I sat down next to him and said, "I don't know but at least you are sober so that you can think more clearly and figure all this out."

"Yeah, a lot of good that does me now! I went into treatment so that this wouldn't happen," said David as he leaned his head back on the couch.

I said, "There were no guarantees. If you hadn't gone into the hospital you might be dead today! You admitted that yourself. And then where would I be?"

David said, "Maybe I should just drink! What the hell is the difference? My life is over any way!"

"Please don't say that," I said. "The kids and I need you, and we need you sober!"

David said, "I can't even talk about this anymore today. I'm exhausted. I need a shower and I'm going to bed."

"What happens tomorrow?" I asked.

"I have to be there every day for the next few weeks to tie up all the loose ends. I have to figure out what I'll do with all the shit there. There's all sorts of paperwork that has to be filled out," said David.

"Okay," I said, "so you have to get up at the regular time then?"

"Yes . . . and that asshole from the fuel company is going to be there every fucking day watching over me to make sure I'm doing what I'm supposed to be. I hate that fucking asshole!"

"He's probably just doing his job, isn't he?" I asked.

"He's a fucking asshole! He loves watching me fail," said David.

As David and I got up from the couch I said, "We will get through this if we put our heads together."

He shook his head, "I don't know how. What do I do when I don't have my business to go to anymore? What the fuck am I going to do then?"

I said, "You will go out and find yourself a new job. That's all. You are a talented mechanic. You will get hired somewhere. You know a lot of people who might be able to give you some good leads."

"I hope you're right," said David, "I'm getting in the shower now. I'm fucking exhausted."

I asked, "Do you want something to eat when you get out?"

David said, "No. I can't eat. I'm just going to bed then."

"Okay," I said.

It was late then but I stayed up after David went to bed and read from my *ONE DAY AT A TIME IN ALANON* again. It had become like my life saver. I could look in the index and find any emotion that I was feeling and find a passage that might help to give me strength.

Tonight I looked up how to help the addict and was very surprised by what I read. I read that sometimes the best thing to do for the alcoholic, recovering or not, is absolutely nothing. Just like Debbie had told me, I needed to let him fix the situation that he'd gotten himself into, by himself. The best thing that I could do for myself was to take care of me and to change the things that I needed to for myself because the only person that I could change was me. That's what I read.

Wow! That's a relief!

I had wasted so much time over the years thinking that I could change him. In fact, I'd thought that it was my responsibility as his wife to help him become the husband and father he should be.

It felt like a huge weight was slowly . . . very slowly, being lifted off of my shoulders as I began to understand fully how powerless I was over anyone but myself.

CHAPTER 15

CAROL WAS CRYING AS SHE told her story, "My husband was out late again a couple of nights ago. He came home early in the morning just reeking of booze and perfume. He makes me sick!"

The Al-Anon group leader, Mary, passed the box of tissues around so that Carol could wipe her eyes.

After she grabbed a tissue, she said, "My son was sleeping, and my husband was falling down drunk all over the place. I just wanted him to be quiet!"

Mary said, "We are all sorry to hear that Carol, and we are here to support you. How did you handle that situation?"

Carol said, "Not well at all. I was so pissed off. He promised me that he would stop just a week ago!"

Mary said, "Maybe it would help you, Carol, to read more about this insidious disease. Your husband probably meant every word when he made his promise but couldn't possibly keep it without his doing something different. Go on though, and tell us the rest of your story. This is the best place for you to unload."

Carol wiped her tears and went on to say, "It only got worse. I couldn't help myself. I slapped him so hard across the face! It didn't even seem to faze him. He just went to bed, and he didn't even remember it the next morning."

Mary asked, "Does anyone want to help Carol with this?"

An old timer at this meeting chimed in. Anna said, "I've been attending these meetings for a long time, Carol. I know I've had some of the same experiences in my life as you are having in yours. It wasn't until I decided to handle myself differently that I could live each new day without guilt. My husband is still drinking to this day as well. He's never even promised to quit but I have chosen to stay with him."

Carol said, "I really do feel so guilty for hitting him. But it got even worse. That's why I'm here today, especially. Last night my husband was out again. I had just gotten my four year old out of the tub and into his pajamas for the night. I asked him to clean up the toys in his room when I got a phone call from my husband and I could hear that he was drunk again. I slammed the phone down on him and went back to my son's room and when I tripped over his toys and hurt my foot, I lost it. He was sitting on the floor and I was leaning over him screaming at him. I mean I really screamed at him. He was cowering on the floor with the most frightened look on his face that I'd ever seen. I could feel that my blood pressure must have been high in that moment . . . my face felt so flushed."

I reached out to Carol who was sitting next to me and took her hand as she continued.

She cried out loud as she said, "And I know what stopped me! I happened to look into the mirror above my son's dresser and I saw myself. I didn't even recognize myself! I looked like a crazy person! He was so scared of me in that moment that it shocked me back into the reality of what I was doing. My reaction was so over the top, and I know now after some thought that it had nothing to do with my son and his toys being a mess. It had everything to do with the anger I was feeling towards my husband."

Mary said, "I think that a lot of us have been there, Carol. We are so happy for you that you were able to stop yourself."

"Oh my God, so am I," Carol said. "I told my son that I was sorry and I cried with him. I feel like I need to apologize to him again and again."

Mary said, "Actions speak louder than words. You can show him by your behavior from this day forward."

Carol said, "As I look back at that moment when I was so out of control, I realize now how a person might abuse their child. It's at that point where I was able to stop myself that maybe an abuser would have just continued. I felt like my Higher Power allowed me to see myself in that moment so that I could stop. I shudder to think what I might have done next!"

I said, "But you didn't, Carol. You stopped yourself. I want to thank you for sharing that story because I think that more than one of us here has been in a similar situation. The difference might be that some of us might not have the courage that you've had today by sharing that with us."

Carol said, "I felt like I had to talk about it. I figured there's less chance of that ever recurring if I just talk about it."

Mary said, "Thanks for being so brave today, Carol. I think you've helped all of us more than you know."

As the meeting concluded that afternoon, I walked out with Carol. Several members stopped her on her way out to give her a hug and to tell her again how brave she was to share her story with all of us.

On our way out the door, I told her the same.

I admitted, "I've gotten just as mad at J.R. as you did at your son. As you were telling that story, I thought that maybe you'd been peeking in my window at my house."

Carol said, "Seriously? I thought I was the only one who felt this crazy out of control!"

"You're not alone, Carol! Not by a long shot!"

"That's really comforting to know," Carol said.

I said, "I wish that I could talk longer but I've got to get home to the babysitter."

Carol said, "Hey, no problem, we'll talk soon."

As I pulled into the garage at home, I was surprised to see David's car there as well. He was home earlier than I'd expected but his schedule had become a bit erratic since the news that his business would be closing.

I found it strange that my babysitter was still in the house. I'd thought that David would relieve her. I noticed that my bedroom door was closed.

Dolores said, "David came home a little while ago but asked me to stay because he was not feeling well. He went to lie down."

I said, "Oh, okay. Let me pay you."

I walked Dolores to the door and said, "Thanks as always for your help. I appreciate it."

Dolores said, "Just give me a call when you need help next, Karen."

"I will, Dolores, thanks again."

I passed the girls in the family room as they watched cartoons and told them, "We will leave in just a few minutes to pick up your brother at school. Get your shoes and coats, okay?"

As I opened my bedroom door to check on David, he was sitting in the recliner chair fully dressed just staring out the window.

I said, "Are you sick?"

David said sarcastically through clenched teeth, "Sick and fucking tired? Yeah!"

"Seriously," I said. "Are you feeling ill?"

He said through clenched teeth, "Not really no, just really pissed off!"

I pretended I didn't notice his foul mood and said, "Okay, well I'm glad that you aren't really sick. I have to go pick J.R. up at school. I'll take the girls with me. We have a few errands to do on the way home."

David said, "Yeah, whatever. Just get the hell out of here. Don't bother me."

His mood was a bit frightening but nothing I wasn't used to, so I helped the girls with their coats and we were off.

I hoped that given a little bit of time alone, that I'd find David in a better mood when I returned.

We arrived back at the house right around dinnertime so I had picked up some fried chicken on the way home for a treat.

I said to them, "Okay, all of you, get your coats off and wash your hands for dinner. I'll set the table."

As they went running off, I realized how quiet the house was otherwise. I got the table set and then went into my bedroom to find David still in the same spot where I'd left him, staring out the window.

I said, "I've got dinner on the table. Are you going to join us?"

David said softly, "I'll be there in a while."

"Okay, come and get it while it's hot."

I sat down at the table with the kids. I filled their plates and got them drinks and sat down to eat with them.

J.R. said, "How come Dad is not eating with us?"

I said, "I think he's not feeling well but he said he will be out to eat soon."

J.R. said with a laugh, "He better hurry or I'm going to eat all the chicken," and as he did so he started doing a chicken dance of sorts in his chair.

We all laughed which made J.R. jump from his chair and do an even more exaggerated dance which involved running in circles and flapping his arms. The girls and I laughed so hard we had tears in our eyes. Leave it to J.R. to be sure we were entertained!

I filled a plate for David and left it by his place at the table. The kids were just finishing up when David walked into the room quietly and sat down at the table.

Gina said, "Can I be done, Mommy?"

I said, "Sure. Please help your sister wash her hands too . . . okay?"

"Okay," she said with a smile. She loved being a big sister to Val since the day she was born. Gina was always older and wiser, way beyond her years.

J.R. said, "I saved you a couple of good pieces, Dad."

"Yeah, yeah," said David.

I started to clean up some of the dishes as David began to eat.

I said, "So what's going on today? Are you okay?"

"I'm just so sick . . . and fucking tired . . . of all this bullshit at the gas station. It seems like it will never end. All the crap I have to take care of. I just don't give a shit anymore!"

My back was to him for a moment while I stood by the sink and when I looked back he was brushing his arm across the kitchen table violently enough to knock his dish and all those that remained right onto the floor with a clatter.

"What the hell!" I said. "What are you doing?"

He stood up with such force that his legs banged into the bottom of the table, almost overturning the whole thing.

He turned, and as he headed out of the kitchen he passed J.R.'s bedroom door and punched it so hard that it left a dent.

I could see that his fist was bleeding as he headed down the hall in the direction of where the kids were. He yelled, "I CAN'T TAKE THIS FUCKING SHIT ANYMORE. I HATE YOU AND THIS FUCKING HOUSE AND MY FUCKING LIFE!"

I dropped what I was doing at the sink to follow him and to get to the kids before he did.

Gina and Val were standing at their bedroom door and as we passed, I grabbed them both by the hands and led them in the direction of the front hall. J.R. was already there. We'd been through this before. We all knew our parts. But this time would be different. God help me, it would be different!

David went into our room as he raged uncontrollably.

"I WANT A FUCKING DIVORCE. I FUCKING HATE YOU!"

The girls were crying by now. I knew what we had to do.

I said to them quietly. "J.R., go in the closet right there. Grab your coat and your sisters' coats. Help them to put them on."

"I could see that David was tearing up our room. He threw the pillows and the blankets out into the hall. He didn't even notice when I slipped by to grab my purse and the car keys.

J.R. pleaded, "I have just my slippers on, Mom!"

"That's okay," I said. "Just help your sisters!"

I had my coat in my arm as David ran out of the bedroom at us. As I stood in front of the kids, David screamed at me, "WHERE THE FUCK DO YOU THINK YOU'RE GOING?"

I said, "J.R., take your sisters out to the car right now! I'll be right there!"

J.R. said in a panicked voice, "Are you okay, Mom?"

David yelled again, "WHERE THE FUCK DO YOU THINK YOU'RE GOING?"

I said, "I'll be right outside J.R.! Get your sisters in the car . . . NOW!"

I yelled at David, "I'M TAKING THE KIDS OUT OF HERE! YOU DO WHATEVER THE HELL YOU NEED TO DO . . . BUT WE ARE NOT GOING TO WATCH ANYMORE!"

David yelled, "FUCK YOU! YOU DON'T GIVE A SHIT ANYMORE! I HATE YOU! GO! GO AHEAD AND GO! I'M GOING TO FUCKING SHOOT MYSELF AND IT WILL BE YOUR FAULT! I'LL BE DEAD WHEN YOU GET BACK!"

David headed back to our bedroom then as I headed for the front door. As I closed it behind me I could hear glass breaking in the house. I ran to the car out front. I slid into the front seat, turned on the ignition and took off!

CHAPTER 16

WHEN I GOT BACK TO the house the next morning after taking J.R. to school, I was so relieved that David was gone! Out of the house!

Thank God!

I settled the girls down with a snack and put on their Zoobilee Zoo tape. The house could fall down around them while that show was on. They loved it so much.

As the theme song played, Gina danced around Val and said, "I love Talkatoo Cockatoo, Mommy!"

I said with a smile, "I know you do, Sweetie, she's great."

"Watch with us, Mommy!" said Gina.

"I have to make a phone call first and then I will," I said.

"Ohhhhhhkay Mommy. I love you," said Gina.

"And I love you too, both of you," I said as we did a group hug.

I smiled at them both. Even Val was mouthing the words to the song all about Mayor Ben and Lookout Bear and all the rest as I went into my bedroom to get the phone.

I couldn't wait to call Debbie.

She answered on the first ring.

"Morning, Debbie," I said.

Debbie said, "Good morning to you Karen, you sound pretty chipper this morning!"

"I have to say I'm feeling pretty proud of myself this morning," I said. "There was an incident here last night with David, and I finally had the courage to do something I'd never done before."

"Tell me all about it," said Debbie.

"I was at an Al-Anon meeting when he came home. My babysitter told me that he had come in and asked her to stay with the kids, that he was not feeling well. He asked her to stay so that he could lie down and rest. I got home and after letting the babysitter go for the day, I went into my bedroom to check on him. He wasn't physically ill at all. He was just in a foul mood as far as I could tell. He just wanted me to leave him alone, so I did."

Debbie said, "Okay, so far so good."

I explained, "I had to pick my son up from school so I took the girls with me. We had some errands to do as well so it was dinnertime by the time I got home. I purposely stayed out hoping that his mood might pass while I was gone."

"That's a good idea, Karen, because just remember . . . it's not your responsibility to change his mood from bad to good. It's all on him. You can only control yourself! And your plate is overflowing there with the kids as well," Debbie said.

"I'm starting to get that, Debbie. So anyway, I had dinner on the table when I invited David to eat with us. He was in the same spot on the same recliner chair in our room staring out the window. He came to the table as the kids were finishing up. As he began to eat, I tried to have a conversation with him and he just blew up again."

"Oh Karen, I'm sorry to hear that," Debbie said. "What happened next?"

I said, "It was a bad one. He knocked the dishes off of the table and then punched my son's bedroom door so hard that it cracked. I could see that his fist was bleeding and dripping on the carpet as he raged through the house."

"Oh my gosh, Karen, what did you do?"

"The kids were panicking by now. The girls were crying so I shuffled all three of them into the front foyer hall where the closet is. We've been through this before. I stood in front of them to shield them as David was throwing things out of our bedroom."

I could hear that Debbie was choked up as she said, "I'm so sorry to hear this, Karen."

I said, "All of a sudden it hit me. We didn't have to tolerate this anymore. I could do something different. I told J.R. quietly to get his coat and the girls' coats out of the closet and to put them on and get outside to the car. When David saw what we were doing he was furious!"

"What did you say, Karen? What did you do?"

"I told him to do whatever he needed to do but we were not going to watch anymore. He told me to go ahead and leave. He told me that he'd be dead when we got back. And as we left, he ran back into our bedroom and as I slammed the front door shut I could hear glass breaking."

Debbie said, "I'm so proud of you, Karen . . . that could not have been easy for you."

I said, "It was one of the hardest things I've ever done. I'm so used to reacting one way and leaving was totally out of character for me and I could see that it really pissed him off. Up until now I've tried to do whatever it takes to prevent that, but I'm realizing now that it's NOT all about him. I have to think of myself and my kids and what's best for us."

Debbie actually laughed then as she said, "All I can say, Karen, is that you must be going to the right Al-Anon meetings because what you did last night took a lot of courage. I know I gained a lot of courage too, by going to a lot of meetings and just listening. You need to be so proud of yourself for daring to make a change like that for yourself and for those kids of yours."

I said, "It really does feel good. I feel like I'm making progress."

Debbie said, "So where did you go with the kids?"

I said, "We took off quickly as soon as I got into the car and when we'd driven a few blocks away, I parked the car to catch my breath. I've found lately that when I get very upset to the point where I can feel my heart racing, I can calm myself by doing some deep breathing. When the kids noticed that I was calming down, so did they. I told them that their dad was having a tough time but we would not have to watch him rage anymore. The solution was simple. If he chooses to behave that way, we'll just leave. We ended up going out for ice cream and then we went to the library."

"Your kids are so lucky to have you, Karen," said Debbie.

"Thanks, Debbie," I said.

"How long did you stay out?" asked Debbie.

I said, "We stayed out for just a couple of hours and when we got back David was sleeping. I could see the damage that he'd done. His armoire had doors that opened at the top. There was a large mirror inside that I could see was broken. There were just a few shards left hanging inside the dresser. It's a shame. It was such a beautiful piece of furniture."

"Yeah, that is too bad," Debbie said, "But that's his issue, not yours."

"You're right," I said, "and you know what else? He actually cleaned up the glass. I could see it all in the garbage can. Normally he leaves all that shit for me to clean up after him."

"I'm sure you've heard this at meetings, Karen. If we as co-dependents change our behaviors, very often the addicted person will make some changes as well, without even thinking about it."

"I have heard that, you're right, Debbie."

Debbie asked, "Did you talk to him this morning?"

"No, I ended up sleeping on the couch and when I got up to get the kids going for the day, he was still sleeping. The girls and I took J.R to school, ran a few errands, and when we got back he was gone, thank God!"

"Tell me Karen, has David been going to any meetings at all for himself?"

"As far as I know, he hasn't made even one meeting since his business went under and that's been about three weeks now," I answered.

Debbie said, "There's not a damn thing you can do about that. Just keep doing what you're doing for yourself. I'm so happy for you and for your kids. The emotional abuse that goes on with dysfunctional families is bound to continue from generation to generation unless someone steps up to the plate and makes huge changes. And that's exactly what you're doing!"

"Thanks Debbie, I will. I have the sitter coming this afternoon, in fact, so that I can get to another meeting with my friend Carol."

"Well good for you! I think you are the greatest, Karen! I'll see you in a couple of days for our next ACG. In fact, if you don't mind, I'd like to sit down alone with you that night. There are just a few personal things I'd like to share with you."

"Sounds great to me, see you then," I said.

As I hung up the phone, I thought about how lucky I was to have my children around me to motivate me to be a better person.

There's a reason for everything.

I was realizing more and more that it was up to me to ensure their well-being, now and for the future. I had to break the chain of abuse, verbal and otherwise if there was going to be any chance of their having healthy relationships in their own lives as adults.

I remember listening to David's father verbally abusing his mother, time after time, while we dated. He was not even shy about the way he spoke to her in front of company. I remember thinking that it was such blatant disregard for her feelings. The way that he spoke to her was just cruel.

I felt so sorry for her.

He'd say things like, "Shut up, Rita! You don't know what the hell you're talking about." Or, "These potatoes taste like shit, what did you do to them?" Or even, "What do you mean you can't do that . . . are you stupid?"

It wasn't until now, that I realized that David talked to me the same way. The only difference was that David didn't say these nasty things to me in front of other people. He might mutter them under his breath, but he didn't let on to people around us that he had such disrespect for me. Everyone thought he was a nice guy and I never let on that he wasn't.

We both learned how to be incredibly talented impersonators.

I was sorry to think that our ACG meetings would be coming to an end soon. They had become my safe haven to talk about what was bothering me without fear of David's violent reaction. I would actually take mental notes when things were uncomfortable and abusive at home, and say to myself that I would confront him with it at our next ACG.

He was so unresponsive to my concerns at home. David's world revolved around David only. When I would try to tell him how I felt about something he would tell me that my feelings were stupid and wrong. Period.

But those are my feelings . . .

David never really acknowledged his behavior from the evening of his last tantrum. I didn't bring it up. I just tried to keep peace in the household for the kids' sake.

The broken mirror in David's armoire was reminder to us all.

On our way to our next ACG though, I was nervous about the topic coming up. It had been so volatile. But I knew I'd done the right thing by admitting to Debbie what had happened. I was sure that it would come up and David would be angry that I'd divulged information about his behavior. But off we went.

We got to the meeting a few minutes early and I just shook my head a bit as David smiled and joked around with a couple of the guys out in the front vestibule of the building. Just as friendly as he could be . . . to everyone but me.

It made me so sad.

I chatted with a couple of friends as well, and when it was almost time for the meeting to begin Debbie walked up to me and said, "Remember, I want to sit down with you for few minutes after the meeting, okay?"

"Yes, sure, no problem," I said.

Debbie said with a smile, "Okay, great!"

As David and I walked into the meeting together, I said to him, "After the meeting, I need to speak to Debbie for a few minutes alone, ok?"

David said quietly, "Sure, now let's get this over with. I'm glad these meetings are almost done. I'm getting tired of coming here."

After everyone was seated Keith addressed the group, "Today we are going to talk about some of the significant changes that take place in one on one relationships as we proceed in our recovery. It was suggested to Debbie and me, early in our recovery, that we focus on ourselves first. And after we had some time to get used to sobriety and all the changes that go along with it . . . only then could we try to come back as a couple to see if we still felt the same way about each other. Sometimes, one person in the relationship might grow and change at a different pace than the other, and in turn the couple grows apart."

All eyes were on Keith.

"We have been in recovery for quite a few years, and we have seen a lot of broken people who are hoping to come back together as a happy and healthy couple. Sometimes it works and sometimes it doesn't. We have seen some couples grow stronger through this whole experience, and we have seen just as many fall apart."

That scares me.

"Some couples realize that they never should have been together at all. They realize in sobriety that they were never meant to be together . . . that there are too many differences to stay together."

What if he leaves me? What if he realizes that we never should have been together at all?

Debbie said then with a laugh, "Okay, Keith, enough about us. Let's go around the room now and see how you all feel about what Keith has said and how it relates to your own recovery."

Dan spoke up right away to say, "I was addicted to cocaine really bad. I'm sober now for 5 months and I'm proud to say that I've been to 5 meetings every week ever since I got out of rehab."

Keith said, "Happy to hear that Dan, good for you."

"My concern," Dan said, "is that my wife is not attending meetings at all. I really want us to recover together and I don't want to take her inventory but I can't help worrying what's going to happen to us if she doesn't do what it takes to recover fully from all the shit I put her through."

"Well said, Dan," said Debbie. "I think you have a valid concern there."

Keith said, "So what's going on with you, Pam?"

Pam said, "I haven't missed any of these meetings here but I am just not comfortable going to Al-Anon or Nar-Anon. I've tried a couple and I just haven't felt like I belonged there. And besides, this is Dan's problem, not mine."

Debbie said, "Seriously? Are you kidding? Do you realize how lucky you are to have a mate who wants you to get well along with him? There are so many more addicts who refuse to do the things that they know will help them to get better just because they're too stubborn to believe that they need any help at all."

"I guess that's true," said Pam.

Keith said, "Karen, I think that you and Pam don't live too far from each other. Have you found any meetings that you like in your area?"

"Actually, yes I have found several," I said. "I'd be happy to share that information with you at the end of the meeting, Pam."

Pam said, "Thanks, I promise I will try a few more meetings."

Debbie said to me then, "Karen, how many meetings have you been attending?"

"I've been attending two a week. That's about all I can fit in with the schedule that I have with my kids!"

Debbie said, "That's great that you've made the time to attend that many. Have they been helpful to you?"

I said, "Very helpful. They seem to be giving me courage to change some things."

"Like what?" said Debbie.

"I've had the courage to react to David's anger differently than I have in the past," I said rather timidly.

Debbie asked, "Can you elaborate on that?"

I knew exactly what she wanted me to talk about, so I did.

"David came home from work in such a foul mood the other day, and when he raged through the house, I realized that I didn't have to stick around and watch like I have for so long."

I didn't even have to turn my head towards David to feel his eyes boring into the side of my head.

Keith asked, "What did you do differently this time, Karen?"

"I got the kids in the car and we left the house for a couple of hours. I told David that we were not going to watch anymore."

All eyes turned to David when Keith said, "What's up with you, David?"

"I was just in a bad mood . . . it was no big deal."

Keith asked me, "Can you be more specific, Karen? What actually happened? Please talk to David directly."

My eyes began to well with tears and I took a deep breath.

No tears! Just tell him! Say it out loud!

I said, "You threw everything off of the dinner table. You punched J.R.'s bedroom door and broke it. You scared the crap out of me and the kids. And you broke the mirror in your dresser into a million pieces."

Keith said, "Wow, you call that no big deal, David? Where's this rage coming from?"

David replied, "My business has failed, my life is shit and I just blew up."

"When's the last time you were at an AA meeting buddy?"

"I went last night," David lied.

Liar, liar, pants on fire.

I couldn't even move in my chair. It was like someone had poured cement in my chair and imprisoned me there. I don't think I was even breathing as Debbie looked at me with that knowing look in her eye. She and I both knew he was lying . . . again.

Keith asked, "Were you able to talk about how you were feeling at the meeting? Did it help you out at all?"

"Yeah, it helped a little," David said.

I could see from the look in Keith's eyes that he doubted David as well.

He asked, "How many meetings have you been able to get to for the last couple of weeks anyway?"

David answered, "I've been going every other day."

Picture a screaming loud siren going off above his head; flashing red lights and all. That's what it felt like, his lies were so obvious.

Keith looked at me directly then and said, "The topic of the night. Recovering people growing together or apart. How's it going for you, Karen?"

"If you are asking me what I think? Here it is," I said. "David's been sober . . . without drugs or alcohol for almost six months now. Nothing besides that has changed. In fact, I think that things between us are even worse than they were when he was drinking and using. I feel like I'm struggling to make some changes for the better. He's doing NOTHING."

There, I said it . . .

And who was I kidding; I'd probably be paying the price soon.

Keith looked me straight in the eyes then and said this slowly, *"Sometimes our hearts won't let us do what our minds tell us we should."*

The hairs on the back of my neck stood straight up . . .

CHAPTER 17

THE WORDS REVERBERATED THROUGH MY head again.

"Sometimes our hearts won't let us do what our minds tell us we should," said Keith again.

I felt like there was no one else in the room then but Keith and me, and that he had slapped me across the face with this obvious message to me.

I knew exactly what he was saying to me without actually saying it.

I felt like his eyes were peering into the darkness in my soul. How did he know what even I was too afraid to say, even to myself? I could not and would not admit defeat.

This is what Keith was actually saying to me in a coded message of sorts. *You are too smart for this relationship, he's a loser, rid yourself of him, it's what your head is telling you that your heart won't let you do.*

I was screaming inside my head!

YOU'RE WRONG! OUR MARRIAGE WILL GET BETTER! DAVID WILL BE KINDER! I JUST HAVE TO BE PATIENT! HE LOVES ME, DOESN'T HE?

All eyes in the room were on me now. I could feel my face was flushed.

Keith said, "You certainly seem to be moving along in your recovery at a much different pace than David. I'm just telling you what I'm observing."

NO! NO! YOU'RE WRONG! WE WILL SURVIVE THIS!

I said, "That's true, yes."

As Keith looked directly at David, he said with just a bit of a grin, "Just a friendly warning to you, David. Karen is a smart and beautiful woman. Frankly speaking, I don't think she's going to tolerate your bullshit for too long."

Oh my God . . .

I could just about see the steam coming out of David's ears as he said, as calmly as he could, "I'm just going through a rough time right now. Karen and I will get through this."

Keith looked right at me again as he said, "You two are a perfect example of what we are discussing tonight . . . two people perhaps growing apart because of a different recovery plan."

"Let's move along now," said Debbie.

I could hear in her voice that she was aggravated but we moved along with the conversation of the night.

Debbie addressed Jeff, "Where's your wife tonight, Jeff? Everything okay?"

Jeff said, "Marie and I just found out that we are going to be new parents! We're ecstatic about it but she's not feeling too well and her doctor advised that she stay off her feet as much as possible for this first trimester."

Debbie said, "How wonderful! We are all so happy for you! Please send her our best."

I was so relieved that the focus was off of me and David for the moment.

The room was abuzz with excitement for Jeff and Marie. The rest of the meeting was just a blur for me. Like David, I could hardly wait to get outside, away from this assault. That's what it felt like.

After I'd had a few minutes to digest what Keith had said, I was feeling angry.

How dare you tell me what to do in my marriage! You don't know what you're talking about! Of course we'll be okay. Of course it will work out.

At that moment I could just about see myself loading the mortar in between the bricks in front of me as I started to put up a wall between me and Keith's suggestion.

I won't listen to that! I can't! We are going to be together for better or for worse!

As the meeting closed, I walked out with Pam and David.

David was as ready as I was to run out of this place. He said, "I'll be in the car."

I said, "Okay."

Pam said, "Karen, are you all right? You look kind of shook up."

I said, "I'm okay I guess. This was a rough one for me."

Pam gave me a great big hug then and said, "None of this recovery shit is easy. I hear ya."

I said, "Why don't you give me your phone number please, and I'll call you tomorrow with the information about the meetings that I've been going to. I can give you addresses and times then, okay?"

"That sounds great, Karen, thanks."

As I looked up I could see that Debbie was waiting for me at the door.

I took a deep breath as I walked up to her. I had an ominous feeling about the conversation before us. She was not smiling but had a look of concern on her face as she said, "Karen, let's scoot on over to my office so we can talk privately for a couple of minutes, okay?"

"Sure," I said.

Debbie held the door open for me and then closed it behind us. There were a couple of chairs facing the front of her desk. She invited me to sit down on one as she sat on the other.

She said, "Karen, I'm not happy about what I'm about to tell you but I feel like I have no choice."

"Okay, what is it?" I asked nervously.

Debbie said, "I feel like I've gotten to know you so well these past few months, and I'm so proud of you for all the growth I've seen in you and your recovery. We've had such great conversations and I've enjoyed so much being your sponsor."

Oh no . . .

Her eyes welled with tears as she continued.

"You and I have talked about so many things. I know how painful it's been for you to be so brutally honest about what's going on between you and David."

"It has been difficult, yes. And I really appreciate your listening to me and your feedback," I said.

"Here's where I have a huge problem. When we are together at these meetings . . . I have to say that I'm about ready to jump out of my chair and just lunge at David when I hear him lying to all of us!"

"I know that you know that he's lying," I said. "It's embarrassing for me."

Debbie said much louder, "He should be embarrassed! Not you! Don't allow him to make you feel that way, Karen. This is totally on him."

As she dabbed the tears from her eyes, Debbie went on to say, "I've really thought about this and I've even talked at length to my own sponsor about this and I just have no choice. I wanted to tell you on the phone the other day, but I thought it would be better face to face. You and I both know that David has been lying to all of us from the beginning and I just can't be a part of it. Tonight's lies just confirmed it for me. So because of that, I can no longer be your sponsor. It breaks my heart but it's just not good for me . . . or for you."

"Oh," I said as I felt a huge lump in my throat.

Wow, talk about slapping the other cheek.

Debbie shook her head from side to side as she said, "I'm truly sorry but I just don't see another way here. I just can't be a part of this."

I said with a huge sigh, "Okay, I hear you."

I need to get outside. I can't breathe.

I stood up then and said, "I gotta go, David's in the car waiting for me."

Debbie stood up then and gave me a big hug.

She said, "I'm really sorry, Karen. I know you've been going to lots of meetings and you talk to a lot of program people. Please don't be discouraged by this. I suggest you choose one of those people to be your new sponsor."

Yeah, whatever.

As I walked to the exit doors, I could feel the tears running down my face. I heard someone calling my name to say goodnight. I didn't even look in their direction. I just had to get outside. I felt like I was being strangled here.

Once again, I'm being punished because of his bullshit! I lose.

As soon as I opened the car door, I was assaulted again.

David yelled "WHO THE FUCK DOES KEITH THINK HE IS TALKING TO ME THAT WAY?"

As I sat in the passenger side of the car, I looked out the window and said quietly, "I don't know, David."

I didn't have it in me to argue with him. I felt like someone had literally beaten the crap out of me. I felt so defeated.

David screamed even louder as he pulled out of the parking lot, screeching the tires as he went; he was going so fast!

"I AM NEVER GOING BACK TO THAT FUCKING MEETING AGAIN! I'VE HAD IT WITH THEIR BULLSHIT! I DON'T KNOW WHO THE FUCK THEY THINK THEY ARE! FUCK THEM AND THE FUCKIN HORSE THEY RODE IN ON!"

As he yelled, David drove even faster. Everything was whizzing by at warp speed as I stared out the window. There was just a little bit of me that hoped we'd make it home safe. I really didn't care that much at that moment. If we got into an accident, maybe David would finally wake up to reality.

"AND YOU! YOU'RE NO BETTER! THIS IS ALL YOUR FAULT! HOW COULD YOU TELL THEM ALL THAT BULLSHIT ABOUT WHAT HAPPENED THE OTHER NIGHT??"

I replied, "I was just being honest."

David yelled more, "HOW DARE YOU TELL THEM EVERY PERSONAL DETAIL ABOUT OUR LIVES! IT'S NONE OF THEIR FUCKING BUSINESS! I REALLY HATE YOU! I'D LOVE TO SHOVE YOU RIGHT OUT OF THAT FUCKING CAR DOOR!"

"I was just being honest," I said again. "It's the only way anything will ever change!"

"YOU CAN BE AS FUCKING HONEST AS YOU WANT! BY YOURSELF! CUZ I'M NEVER GOING BACK THERE AGAIN!"

"I heard you," I said.

He slowed down the car just a little on the highway and swerved to the right side of the road, and while he was still moving he screamed at me, "JUST GET OUT OF THE FUCKING CAR NOW BEFORE I FUCKING THROW YOU OUT!"

"WHAT, ARE YOU CRAZY?" I yelled.

"YOU WANT TO SEE CRAZY . . . I'LL FUCKING SHOW YOU CRAZY! GET OUT OF THE FUCKING CAR NOW!"

"NO!" I yelled.

He drove down the emergency lane for at least a mile. I could hear the gravel spitting up at the car because of the speed.

After what seemed like several minutes, he drove back on the main part of the road and drove even faster. As he swerved back into traffic, our car almost hit another car next to us. The man in the other car laid on his horn and opened his window to scream at David, which just pissed him off even more.

David pushed the button to open his window and screamed out the window at the other driver, "FUCK YOU!"

From where I sat, I could read the speedometer. We were going eighty five miles an hour.

"SLOW DOWN! YOU'RE GONNA KILL US BOTH!" I yelled.

Dear God, just get me home safe to my kids.

I was frozen in my seat then . . . I had moved right up against the door and was holding onto the door handle, just waiting for the impact.

Am I really crazy or do you seem to get off on terrifying me?

※―※―※

He never even asked me what Debbie had wanted. David just didn't give a shit about anyone but himself. As my eyes began to open to my reality, I became more and more aware of just how selfish David was and always had been.

The world revolved around David and David only.

We did manage to get home in one piece that night and as I relieved the babysitter and walked her to the door, David went into our bedroom and went right to sleep.

The quiet was such a relief. I turned the TV on softly and sat up on the couch for hours thinking and reading from my *ONE DAY AT A TIME* book.

I read, *I can live my life only one day at a time. Perhaps my confusion and despair are so great that I will have to take it one hour at a time, or one minute at a time, reminding myself constantly that I have authority over no life but my own.*

That night I felt totally defeated . . . physically and mentally.

And I couldn't get Keith's words out of my head.

Sometimes our hearts won't let us do what our minds tell us we should.

Surely, I would stay with David.

I have no other option. Do I?

He would get better if I was just patient with him . . . wouldn't he?

I worried so much about what might happen so I read, *If I live just this one day at a time, I will not so readily entertain fears of what might happen tomorrow. If I'm concentrating on today's activities, there will be no room in my mind for fretting and worrying. I will fill every minute of this day with something good. Then when the day is ended, I can look back on it with satisfaction and serenity.*

After a restless night of sleep on the couch, I was clear about a couple of things.

I dialed Debbie's phone number.

She said, "Karen, we were worried about you and David last night. Did you get home all right?"

"Yes, we did . . . just barely. I'm calling to let you know that you shouldn't expect to see David and me anymore at the ACG. We only had two sessions to go anyway and David is totally refusing even the thought of returning."

Debbie said, "I'm sorry to hear that, Karen. Are you sure you don't want to attend on your own?"

I said, "There's really no point . . . no. I'm going to continue going to my Al-Anon meetings. I'll be fine."

"I appreciate your letting us know," said Debbie.

"Hey, no problem," I said.

Debbie said, "You know I love ya, Karen, and I wish you nothing but the best. I'd love to hear from you occasionally to see how you're doing."

"I'll keep in touch. I'll talk to you soon."

As I hung up the phone, I felt calmer than I had in a while. My recovery was all up to me now. I didn't have to even think about arguing with David to get him to attend.

His recovery was up to him. Mine was up to me. Period.

I knew I could do it. I knew I could get stronger. I knew I could become more independent. My children were my strength.

But I'm afraid. So afraid . . .

CHAPTER 18

WE ARE SUCH CREATURES OF habit. It's easy to keep doing what we're doing even if it results in misery. Change is difficult . . . sometimes almost impossible. I was determined though, that I would transform myself into a person that had their shit together, not unlike some of the recovering family members that I'd met at meetings. I was determined that I would have a better life for myself and for my children.

So I kept going to Al-Anon meetings whenever I could. I heard so many things that gave me hope. I had to remind myself daily that the only person I could control was me. I read that if I devoted myself to correcting my own shortcomings and mistakes, it could not possibly have an adverse reaction on David. He had the same right and obligation to work out his own problems as I had to work out mine.

My friend Carol and I went to a lot of meetings together. I was so impressed with so many of the people that I met there.

Rose was a woman who I'll never forget. She was the leader of the group that afternoon, when Carol and I walked in together.

She greeted us at the door, "Good afternoon! I haven't seen your faces here before. Welcome."

Carol and I said our hellos and wandered over to the table full of literature until the meeting began.

Rose started out the meeting by saying, "Welcome to all of you today. Thanks for being here. I know it's not always easy for a lot of us to get here physically and emotionally." She looked in our direction as she said further, "We have a few new people here today and we'd like to make you feel especially welcome."

As I listened, I counted twelve people around the circle of chairs. There were eight women and four men.

Rose said, "The topic for today is beginnings. For new people, this is a great way for all of us who have been here for a while to get to know you. And for those of us who have been here for longer, it's really great to think back at how we started! It's an eye opening indication of how far we have come because of this program, and even more importantly because of the people we have encountered here. You just never know how much you might be helping others when you choose to share your stories. No question there is strength in numbers."

All eyes were on Rose. There was something about the way that she spoke. She was so poised and confident.

Rose said, "I'll start for those of you who don't know my story. I've been attending Al-Anon meetings for about three years now . . . ever since the accident that changed my family's life forever. My husband is my alcoholic. He's been drinking heavily ever since I met him twelve years ago. We have three children together."

Her every word just drew me in. She commanded my attention.

"Three years ago, my husband was driving drunk. He was heading home late one night and fell asleep at the wheel. He had a head on collision with another car. It killed the driver. The man he killed was a new father and a doctor . . . such a tragic loss. My husband was in the hospital for a couple of months and is reminded of this tragedy every day. He lost his right leg in the accident."

As I looked next to me at Carol, I could see that she had tears in her eyes. I wasn't the only one.

Rose went on to say, "Needless to say, that was my wake up call. It's changed my life. I'm still married to him. That's a choice that I've made. What keeps me sane are these meetings and my friends in this program who support me."

Wow, what courage you have. I thought my story was bad. There's always someone out there who is worse off than me.

Rose was just so cool and calm and collected.

I spoke up then and asked, "How do you live with that? You seem so calm. I'm shocked. I don't know how I could get through even one day with that on my mind."

Rose smiled and replied, "It took some time for me to get to this point. I was a total wreck when it first happened. I thank God for my friend, Helen, who was already attending Al-Anon meetings. She encouraged me to give it a try and I'll be forever grateful to her for that. I don't know where I'd be without this."

I asked, "Do you mind telling us? Is your husband still drinking?"

Rose answered with a sigh, "He stopped for about six months after the accident and then he started again. He doesn't work anymore. He's on disability, so now he does all his drinking at home. The only time he goes out is to pick up his liquor. And he walks to the store, because I certainly won't buy it for him."

One of the men in the group spoke up then and said, "Every time I've heard you tell that story, Rose, I'm amazed at your courage. Thanks for sharing that."

Rose said, "You're welcome, Tom. So now you all know about my beginnings here. Who else would like to share?"

Tom said, "I'll go next. I first attended an Al-Anon meeting about two years ago. I had grown up with addictions. My father was an alcoholic and my mother was addicted to prescription medication. Turned out that my wife is an addict as well, or should I say my ex-wife. I still love her but I felt like I had no choice but to divorce her. She's hit rock bottom but unfortunately she doesn't see it. Our divorce will actually be final next week. I came into the program not knowing what to do with my life. I was so uncertain. Immersing myself into Al-Anon meetings and reading as much as I could about the disease helped me to come to the realization that we could not be together anymore. I couldn't watch her self- destruct."

Carol asked, "How long were you married, Tom?"

Tom replied, "We were married for twelve years."

"Any children?" I asked.

"We tried early on. But it never happened for us. It seemed like that was one of the major reasons why she turned to alcohol," said Tom.

I asked, "How did you know for sure that divorce was the right thing to do?"

Tom answered, "I didn't know what to do when I first came to Al-Anon. I felt so lost and alone. But those feelings passed when I had a dozen meetings under my belt. I felt such a fellowship with the people here. And once I felt more confident about myself, the answer came to me. I knew in my heart that it was the right thing to do. I had to start thinking about myself."

"I envy you," I said. "I don't think I would ever have the courage."

"Never say never. Give yourself some time in the program, Karen. If you apply what you learn here, you will become more confident and you will know what to do for yourself."

"Thanks, Tom, for sharing your story," I said.

Still another woman spoke up and said, "My name is Sara, for those of you who don't know me. I've been coming to Al-Anon now for a few months. I began as soon as I realized that my boyfriend was addicted not only to alcohol but to several illicit drugs. We've been living together for one year now and as soon as I realized what a problem it was for him, I gave him an ultimatum. He had a choice. He could go into treatment and stop using or he could move out. I'd never been exposed to this insanity before in my life and I wasn't about to start."

Tom asked, "What did he choose?"

Sara replied, "He actually went into a thirty day program and got sober."

"That's great," said Tom. "How is that going?"

"It has started out pretty well and as far as I can tell, I've seen no signs that he's using but he's not going to meetings. He's not really doing anything to change the things that he should. His behavior is still just as outrageous and volatile as it was when he was using. He loses his temper often and it's always extreme, sometimes over nothing at all."

Rose chimed in than and said, "It sounds like he may be a dry drunk."

I asked, "What the heck is that?"

Rose answered, "A dry drunk is someone who stops drinking or using drugs for that matter, but they don't replace that behavior with something positive to fill the void. So everything remains the same except for the actual substance.

Needless to say, it's just as miserable . . . if not more so than when they used. If you look over at our literature table, we do have a brochure that explains further about dry drunks."

I said, "Thanks, Rose. I will take that one home with me to read. I think that might be going on with my husband too."

As she smiled at Sara and then back at me, Rose said, "Sara, thanks so much for sharing that. It seems it's already helped someone else in the group here. This is exactly how this program works. We can listen to each other and take what we like with us and use it, and leave the rest."

As the meeting closed, we all stood and said the Serenity Prayer together.

Carol said, "Karen, have you got time to go for coffee today?"

"Yes! I'd love to. How about if I meet you at Georgios?"

Carol replied, "Sounds great, I'll see you there."

When we sat down at what was soon becoming our favorite restaurant, we both ordered coffee and pie.

I laughed as I said, "I'm going to have to be careful here. This is becoming a habit. I love their pie here and it goes just perfectly with the coffee, yeah?"

Carol laughed too and said, "I hear ya."

I said, "I'm anxious to read more about this *dry drunk* thing. I hope you don't mind. Can I read it out loud to you?"

"Of course you can. The more I know the better," answered Carol.

I read, "*Unfortunately when many former drinkers go through the grieving process over the loss of their old friend, the bottle, some never get past the anger stage. It's a very real loss. The drink has been their friend for many years and one they could count on. When the world turned against them, the bottle never let them down. It was always there ready for the good times, the celebrations, the parties, as well as the sad, mad and lonely times too.*

Finally their old friend let them down. They got into trouble, lost a job, almost lost their family, or the doctors told them they had to stop using . . . whatever the reason, the circumstances of their life brought them to the point where they made a decision to say so long to the bottle.

Whether they realized it or not, they began the stages of grieving . . . denial, anger, bargaining, depression, and acceptance. Those are the same stages most people go through when they have a great loss in their lives or have been told they have a terminal illness.

First comes the denial. 'It's really not that big a deal. I've always said I can quit anytime.' And then the anger and depression when they realize just how much they have come to depend on their old friend alcohol. Many make it through the process to the final stage; accepting the loss, learning and growing through the experience and moving on.

Some never make it. It's sad to see them, sometimes many years later, still stuck in their anger, bitterness and resentment at having to make the change in their lives. They haven't had a drink in years but they have also never had a 'sober' day.

You can even see them in the 12 step rooms . . . been in the program for years and years and their lives seem to be a constant unmanageable struggle. All those years and they have no more of a spiritual awakening than they did the first time they walked into the room.

Dry Drunk has been described as a condition of returning to one's old alcoholic thinking and behavior without actually taking a drink. Those who quit drinking but are still angry about it wind up living miserable lives and usually make everyone else around them miserable too. If it has been said once in an Al-Anon meeting, it has been whispered thousands of times, 'I almost wish he would go back to drinking.'"

Carol said, "Wow, that's interesting!"

I said, "Yeah, pretty depressing too. What's the point in quitting if it's not going to make you feel better?"

"That is a sad prospect," Carol said. "Maybe it will pass for David?"

"I sure hope so. He's been miserable to live with. I can't let him bring me down. I'm determined to feel better myself. I'm going to do whatever it takes."

Carol said, "Maybe you can talk to him about it?"

I said, "I don't think so. I have to stop taking his inventory and just start taking care of me. If I brought it up to him, I'm sure it would only end up in an argument. And there are enough of those without me stirring another one up."

"I hear you," said Carol.

I said, "But at least having read this, I have a better understanding of what's going on with him even though there's nothing I can do about it. Knowledge is power, yeah?"

"I agree with you totally, Karen," said Carol.

The waitress came to the table with our pie.

I said, "Yum, yum . . . let's dig in girlfriend! There's something else I wanted to talk to you about."

Chapter 19

"Seriously?" asked Carol. "Do you really think we could pull it off?"

"I do. I've been in Al-Anon now for almost a year. You started right around the same time as me and I think I'm ready as long as I have someone like you to help me."

I'd been thinking lately that I'd like to start a new Al-Anon group right in my local parish.

Carol asked, "Where would the meeting take place?"

I replied, "I think that there might be space enough to have a meeting somewhere in one of the buildings by the school my kids go to, right in my neighborhood. What do you think, Carol?"

Carol laughed and replied, "I think that you're pretty ballsy to propose such a thing and I think that I'm proud to call you my friend!"

I laughed and said, "Can I take that as a yes? That you will help me?"

"Absolutely . . . I'll help you. Just let me know what I can do."

I was excited at the prospect, "Wonderful! Thanks Carol. I just feel like the more I get involved with Al-Anon, the better off I'll be. The first thing I'm going to do is to call the Pastor at my church and set up an appointment with him to see if he will agree to letting us use their space."

"That sounds good, Karen. I live pretty close by too. I'm sure there's a need for it. I haven't found enough meetings listed in our area."

I said, "After we get a space, I think all we need is a coffee pot and some Al-Anon Literature and we can get started."

"Awesome!" Carol replied.

I said, "As soon as I get Father Ed's permission, I'll give you a call and we'll talk details . . . okay?"

Carol said, "Sounds great to me! I gotta get going. I have to pick up my son."

As I looked at my watch I said, "Me too. Gotta go."

David managed to tie up all the loose ends at his gas station within a few months of losing it. It had been many years since he'd worked for someone else so the job hunt was a challenge for him.

David was sitting in front of the TV when I said, "It's been five months without a paycheck David. How am I supposed to pay the bills?"

David replied, "Do whatever you gotta do. Just take care of it."

"I've already used all the savings we had. What do you suggest?"

He replied, "If you have to, just use the credit cards to get us by. I hope I'll hear from one of the places I've applied to very soon."

"How long do you think it might be?" I asked.

"I have no idea," he replied, as he looked back in the direction of the TV.

I said, "Maybe in the meantime, you could get a job anywhere . . . doing anything. Fast food place, grocery store . . . anything. We need the money!"

David said, "I'm not doing that! They don't pay shit."

"Your unemployment runs out in a couple of weeks," I said.

He said, "Do you think I don't know that? I'm doing the best I can! Why don't you apply for food stamps?"

I replied, "Could you take care of that? I've got a million things to do today. I'm taking the girls with me now to pick J.R. up from school."

He never did apply for food stamps and after several more months with no paycheck we ended up having to file a personal bankruptcy. It was the only way we could keep our home.

Rita helped us a bit financially. I was a hairdresser at home and was always able to make a few bucks that way. I'd have Valerie in her playpen next to me while I worked. We scraped by.

When even more time passed without him bringing home a paycheck, I got on the phone and set up an interview for myself. One of us had to work.

I said to David, "I have an interview set up. Because of all my years of experience, the owner of the beauty shop is pretty flexible as far as hours go. Which hours will work for you to watch the kids?"

"I can't watch the kids," said David.

I asked, "What do you mean?"

David answered, "I have to keep my schedule free for job interviews and the like."

"Seriously?" I asked him.

"Yeah, seriously. You'll have to figure out a schedule for the kids," David said.

I asked him, "How about Saturdays?"

David replied, "I guess I can watch them on Saturdays."

So I got a job during the hours that J.R. was at school and I put the girls into daycare a couple of days a week. They hated it . . . and so did I. I longed to be home with the three of them where I belonged.

That first Saturday at my new job came, and David told me, "My mom is coming over today."

I asked, "While I'm at work?"

"Yes."

"Why is she coming over while I'm at work?"

David said, "She's going to help me babysit."

With a puzzled look I asked him, "Why do you need your mother to help you babysit your own children?"

"I was talking to her on the phone and she thought that it was a good idea. I didn't want to argue with her so I said it would be okay," David answered.

So that's how it went. Every Saturday Rita would come over to help David. In other words . . . he sat on the couch while she took care of the kids. It was totally frustrating to me. I found that I was still taking care of all the household chores that needed to be done. David was not pitching in while he was not working . . . not one bit.

When I realized that my working may have been allowing him to take even longer to find a job, I quit after a few months. I told my boss that it just wasn't working out for my children and me.

I read this in my ODAT Book. *Of course I am obligated, by compassion and a common humanity, to help others. But this does not mean I should do for them what they ought to do for themselves. I have no right to deprive anyone else of the challenge to meet his own responsibility. Although mutual dependence is one of the comforts and rewards of marriage, each partner must do his own job and carry his own share of the burden. If the alcoholic member of the family fails in his duties, my assuming them will only weaken his will to accept his share of the responsibility.*

So I gave it back to him.

David had applied as an auto mechanic at several car dealers. Finally, he got calls from a couple of places and after interviewing for those positions, he was able to choose the one he wanted.

I was hopeful again. I was patient with him. I was as supportive as I could be. And I tried not to take his inventory. I was focused on myself and my children.

There were constant reminders though, that his business had failed. I found out that he'd cheated the government of their due taxes. Because of that, the IRS contacted us frequently about when we would pay them back what was due them. They threatened to take our home from us.

They tormented us. I was scared to death until I finally realized that they couldn't take anything from us that was really important anyway . . . they couldn't take my kids.

We did the best that we could to stall them. We constantly filled out paperwork for them that proved that if we were to make any kind of payments to them that our children would not have the basic necessities to live every day.

I even wrote a letter to the President asking that we be given a second chance. The IRS actually referred to my letter once when they called me on the phone. Unfortunately I was just as responsible as David for the debt because I was married to him.

There was an IRS agent who actually came to my home and worked in my basement combing through all the files that David had from the gas station. Can you even imagine the humiliation? And I was the one having to keep an eye on them. David was never home when they were there.

It wasn't until ten years later that the threat finally disappeared. The statute of limitations ran out and they couldn't legally try to collect the money from us anymore.

❊-❊-❊

Carol and I did start the new Al-Anon group in our parish. Father Ed was completely agreeable.

I called Carol to let her know the good news. She picked up on the first ring.

"Carol, he said yes! We can start having meetings in the school library as soon as we are ready!"

Carol said, "Oh my gosh, that's great! I'm so excited! What's next? How can I help?"

I said, "Can you come over this week sometime? We can drive together to the main Al-Anon office and browse through the literature and bring some back with us."

Carol asked, "Do we have to pay for it?"

I said, "I made a phone call and found out that they will actually give us a starter kit since we are forming a new group. It includes several different brochures. It will cost a few bucks after that when we order literature."

"Who's going to pay for that?"

"You probably remember that at the meetings we've been at, they pass around a basket for donations."

"Oh, yeah, I do remember," said Carol.

I said, "We will pass around a basket at our meetings every week, and the money will be used for literature and books and coffee supplies."

Carol laughed then and said, "What if no one shows up?"

I laughed and said, "Well, I guess that's possible but we are going to advertise the best that we can and hope for a good turnout."

Carol said, "Just tell me what you need me to do."

"Okay, we can have the room on Wednesday nights so I'll make up some flyers advertising it, and we can drop them off all over the area. Most of the small local stores have bulletin boards we can post on. I can give you some when I see you next."

"That's a great idea. I'll be happy to do that," said Carol. "Maybe I can drop some off at the library?"

I said, "That sounds great. Father Ed had me talk to his secretary too. She's in charge of the ads that go into the church bulletin. They are going to announce the fact that a new Al-Anon meeting is starting there. It will be in the bulletin every week for the next four weeks."

Carol said, "Great! That should help a lot."

We held the first meeting about three weeks later. We were ready to go. Coffee pot plugged in, literature laid out on the table and about twenty chairs lined up in a circle. We were feeling optimistic. All we needed was people.

And then they started to arrive . . . in droves. We were giddy with excitement.

Carol whispered to me, "Oh my God, the meeting doesn't even start for fifteen minutes and we're running out of chairs! This is great!"

I laughed and said, "I guess there was a need for this, huh?"

I met some of the best people there and became lifelong friends with some of them.

There were about six of us that would go to Georgios after each meeting for coffee and dessert. We had some great conversations there. We laughed together and we cried together.

We were there so regularly that our favorite waitress would save our table for us at the same time each week.

I was approached by an old timer at one of my meetings.

Sue said to me, "Karen, I work at the main Al-Anon office in Chicago. There's just two of us who answer the phones. We are only open during the day from nine in the morning til five in the afternoon. We have been overwhelmed with phone calls there. There are people phoning in at all hours of the day and night looking for help. Most of them just need information about where they can find their own local meeting."

"Okay," I said.

Sue said, "You are just the kind of person we are looking for. You are so personable. We need volunteers to pick up the calls and get this information out. Do you think that you could help us out?"

I said, "Tell me more. Can I do it from home?"

"Yes, absolutely. All you have to do is call the office number and I'll give you a code to punch in and the recorder will play that day's messages for you. You phone those people back with the information they need. There's a directory that I can give you a copy of. It lists all the Chicago land meetings and other helpful phone numbers that will come in handy when you assist these people."

"How often would you need me to do this?" I asked.

Sue replied, "You tell me what's good for you."

I said, "Well, let me start out with one day a week and I'll see how that works for me, okay?"

"That would be great," said Sue. "I'll bring everything you need to this meeting next week. Thanks so much."

I said, "No problem, I am happy to help out!"

Sue answered, "You will be so surprised at how rewarding you will find this venture. There are so many people out there who are feeling just as alone and afraid, as you and I did, before Al-Anon, and they are so grateful for our returning their calls for help."

While J.R. was at school and the girls were napping, I would check the phone calls so far for that day. I can remember especially one woman I spoke to.

When she picked up her phone, I said, "Hello, is this Sally?"

"Yes it is," she replied.

I said, "My name is Karen, and I'm calling from the Al-Anon help line."

I could barely get the words out as she interrupted and said, "Oh my God! I'm so glad that you called back right away! I need help in a big way!"

I said, "That's what we're here for. How can I help you?"

"I think I'd better get to an Al-Anon meeting and I'd better go soon!"

I replied, "You sound pretty desperate, Sally."

She said, "I AM!! I'm afraid if I don't get some help right now . . . I'm just gonna kill him! That's all there is to it!"

I said, "Try to calm down, Sally. Maybe I can help you through this. You don't want to kill anyone . . . I'm sure."

"OH YES I DO! I'M SO SICK OF HIS BULLSHIT, I'M JUST GONNA RUN HIM OVER WITH MY CAR! HE'S LEAVING ME NO CHOICE!"

Wow.

I replied, "Now Sally . . . I'm really glad that you and I are talking now. Let's just talk for a few minutes. Maybe I can help you calm down."

She said louder, "YOU DON'T UNDERSTAND! HE'S SUCH AN ASSHOLE AND I WARNED HIM! I TOLD HIM IF HE CAME HOME DRUNK JUST ONE MORE TIME THAT I WAS GONNA KILL HIM!"

I said, "Sally! I do understand. I'm like you. My husband is an alcoholic and a drug addict. I know how you feel. I really do."

Sally said, "He couldn't be as bad as mine! I warned him!"

"Take a deep breath Sally . . . take a couple. You don't want to become violent, do you? Really? I want you to stop and think about what you are feeling. Do you think that this disease and everything that goes along with it, is what's making you feel so crazy?"

I could hear Sally sigh loudly as she said, "Maybe."

I said, "I'm on the outside listening to you and I understand. I'm sure that you don't really want to hurt anyone . . . but I can hear that you do need help right away. Why don't you tell me where you live and I'll look in my directory here for you and find you a meeting where you can go and talk to other people who are going through similar situations."

Sally said, "Okay. I'm trying to calm down. What will happen there? I've never been to a meeting like this."

I answered just the same as I'd been answered the first time I inquired about Al-Anon.

"Al-Anon is a safe place for you to go and vent about what's happening in your life . . . the things that seem so out of control because of the disease of addiction. More importantly, by listening to others in similar situations, you will hear new ideas that will help you to cope and to move forward in your own life without being so controlled by your partner's behaviors. I promise . . . it will make you feel less crazy and more empowered. That's what it's done for me."

"Seriously?" Sally asked. "All of that at a meeting?"

"Seriously," I replied. "In fact, I'll give you the information that you need for several meetings . . . different locations with different people. If you don't find comfort in the first one . . . try another and another still . . . until you feel like you are being helped. That's what I did. And I can tell you it works."

Sally said, "Okay Karen. I'm going to trust you. Where can I find these meetings?"

I found several meetings within a couple of miles from Sally.

I was paying it forward and it felt great!

CHAPTER 20

THE YEARS JUST FLEW BY. My life was so full. I worked really hard at keeping a nice house, cooking, and cleaning, and decorating. Not to mention all the work that goes along with helping the kids with homework, taking them to their after school activities and their doctor visits. I felt like a chauffeur some days and I loved it. It was exactly what I should have been doing. And it kept my mind off of the fact that my marriage was a facade.

I felt stronger emotionally because of Al-Anon. It became my safety net. The friendships at the meetings gave me the strength and the courage to get through each day. And many of the people I met became true friends who I knew I could call anytime for encouragement and support . . . and I did. I could say things to Al-Anon people that I could never admit to *outsiders*.

Al-Anon was like my life boat. I went to at least one meeting every week religiously.

I had become good friends with Pam from the ACG. She and Dan moved out of town and when she came back to visit, we talked and planned on attending a meeting together. I woke up that morning feeling really lousy. I'd detected some pain in my left ear the night before and when I woke up it was a full blown ear ache. I could tell that I needed some medical attention. I mean it was really bad. It felt like the fourth of July going off in my ear and it was actually draining, a mixture of blood and pus. But I opted to go and see my friend Pam and to go to a meeting with her.

I held a tissue to my ear to catch the drainage during the meeting.

Pam looked at me and said, "Are you okay, Karen? What's wrong?"

I replied, "I have a really bad ear ache, that's all."

She said, "Why are you here? Shouldn't you be seeing your doctor for that?"

"I'm here because I needed a meeting and I wanted to be here with you, girlfriend. I've missed you and I know you are going back home tomorrow!"

Pam said, "You have to take care of that, Karen. I appreciate you being here with me though! You are such a good friend!"

At the end of the meeting, I gave Pam a big hug goodbye, and then drove myself over to the emergency room of our local hospital.

When the ER doctor looked into my ear, he said, "Oh my God, you have a horrible infection! Why didn't you seek medical attention sooner?"

I replied, "This was just the soonest that I could get here."

That's how important Al-Anon meetings became to me . . . my lifeline.

My whole outlook on life began to change. David remained stuck. He remained the same.

The kids and I developed our everyday routine. It did not include David. We got used to going just about everywhere without him.

He would show up for major events, mostly because I would insist. He wanted to keep up appearances, so he would comply.

I remember marching into church every week with J.R., Gina, and Val. We'd sit in the front row. I'd look at all the families that looked more normal than us . . . moms and dads and their kids. A friend of mine sat across from us in the front row as well. She sat in between her husband and her son. Her husband was holding their baby daughter. He was nuzzling with her during the church service. She smiled back at him as he kissed her cheek. I could see the love in their eyes.

I envied my friend . . . extremely. How I wished that I had a husband who was kind and gentle with our children. David didn't know how to show emotion. He never had. He never verbalized that he loved them. It made me so incredibly sad.

I had to be mom and dad to all three. That's why I was put here on earth. My most important role in this lifetime was to care for and raise my children. That was always my first focus. I had to love them enough for the two of us. I had to make up to them what they didn't get from David.

David kept a job but he was white-knuckling it. He attended no AA meetings. He had terrible mood swings. He'd fly off the handle at ridiculous every day stuff. I walked around on eggshells most of the time when David was home and so did the kids. This became our normal.

He was depressed, often times felt suicidal. He frequently threatened that he would shoot himself, that it would bring a halt to all his problems. I begged him to get help . . . see a psychiatrist or counselor. He refused.

I knew that I couldn't make him do anything.

David owned a couple of guns. When he had gone into treatment, I'd convinced Rita to get them out of my house but without my knowing, she had returned them to David shortly after . . .

Unthinkable.

I was shocked to say the least. I'd confided in her the fact that David threatened suicide often.

I didn't tell her about all the nights he had come home during the drinking days when he would threaten to shoot me, to be rid of me.

How can I ever forget that? I never will.

I couldn't convince him to get rid of the guns.

"I don't think it's a good idea to have these guns, David," I said.

David replied, "I don't really care what you think. I like having them and that's that."

I said, "It's not safe to have them in the house. I hate guns. Can we please get rid of them?"

He yelled, "NO! THOSE ARE MINE. I WON'T GET RID OF THEM!"

"What if the kids were to find them? Why do we have them here? What good are they?"

"If anyone tried to break into our house, you'll be glad that I have them!" he insisted.

"I'm begging you, David! Please get rid of them! Get them out of the house!"

David replied, "NO! AND DON'T YOU DARE TAKE THEM OUT OF THIS FUCKING HOUSE! YOU UNDERSTAND? THIS FUCKING CONVERSATION IS OVER!"

At least I was able to convince him to hide them in the basement up in the ceiling tiles. I didn't want the kids to know that we had any guns. I was totally against it but David didn't care. My opinion just didn't matter at all. When David wasn't aware, I took the bullets and hid them in the garage. I can remember that my hands trembled as I did so when no one was around, just thinking about his reaction. I thought about the confrontation that might occur if he were looking for them. But I had to protect the rest of us in the house, as best I could anyway.

I'd say, "I know you're not feeling well, David. I can see you're not happy. Your moods are so extreme. Maybe you could talk to a doctor about it. Maybe there's medication that will keep you on a more even keel."

David refused and yelled, "THERE'S NOTHING FUCKING WRONG WITH ME! IT'S JUST THAT NOTHING IS GOING MY WAY LATELY. THE OTHER GUYS AT WORK GET ALL THE GOOD FUCKING JOBS! I CAN'T FIGURE OUT WHY THEY KEEP GIVING ME THE FUCKING SHIT WORK! I CAN'T MAKE MONEY DOING THIS ANYMORE!"

The verbal abuse continued . . . the screaming and yelling and intimidation. It never went away with sobriety. I became numb to the pain. It became my every day until I hardly recognized it as such anymore.

Sometimes our hearts won't let us do what our minds tell us we should.

This thought creeped into my head from time to time but I just kept shoving it down.

You are wrong Keith! I need to stay with him. It's the right thing! Could I even survive without him? I can't even remember my life pre-David!

David's relationship with our children was nonexistent. There were never any meaningful conversations between them. David was too busy in his own head to ever open up to them. He just didn't know how and didn't care enough to figure it out.

By high school age, J.R. really needed his dad more than ever. I could only do so much as his mom. J.R. started to get into trouble . . . the kind of trouble that teenage boys get into when they don't have a father to guide them.

David only showed up, emotionally speaking, to scream at J.R. when he was in trouble.

J.R. had gotten into a physical fight with another teenage boy. He had been extremely aggressive. I got a phone call from the other boy's mother who was screaming at me. She told me that they were considering pressing charges against J.R. This wasn't the first time that he was in trouble with the law, not by a long shot.

It became a screaming match again when David found out. And the screaming matches just led to more aggressive behavior on both of their parts, often times between David and J.R.

David yelled at him, "WHAT THE FUCK IS WRONG WITH YOU? WHAT WERE YOU THINKING?"

J.R. shouted back, "YOU WEREN'T THERE! YOU DON'T KNOW WHAT YOU'RE TALKING ABOUT! I HAD NO CHOICE!"

David shouted, "WHAT IF YOU GET ARRESTED?"

J.R. yelled back, "WHAT IF I DO? WHAT DIFFERENCE DOES IT MAKE?"

"YOU SMART ASS!" David screamed. "KAREN, GET MY GUN! I'M GONNA SHOOT THIS FUCKING SMART ASS!"

J.R. lifted his fist like he was winding up to punch David.
I got right in between them. "STOP IT!"

David pushed me and said, "GET THE FUCK OUT OF
MY WAY!"

I yelled, "J.R., YOU HAVE TO GET OUT OF HERE!
GO TAKE A WALK! THIS CAN'T HAPPEN HERE!"

The girls were hiding in their room, listening at the door.
Gina had grabbed the cordless phone and had dialed 9-1 . . .
and was ready to dial another 1 when she thought it necessary.

J.R. backed away, put on his shoes and was out the front
door without a word.

This kind of confrontation happened frequently.

I know now that part of the reason for J.R.'s crazy
behavior was his desperate attempt at getting his dad's
attention. It didn't work. It never happened.

On another day, there was a big argument between J.R.
and Gina. It became physical. Valerie had been a witness to the
whole thing and she was crying hysterically. It was late at
night. I was already in bed.

Valerie came storming into my bedroom.

"MOM! J.R. IS FIGHTING WITH GINA! YOU
HAVE TO GET UP! DAD IS USELESS!"

I shook myself awake and ran down the stairs to where all
the ruckus was. I could hear Gina crying and J.R. and David
yelling at each other.

J.R. yelled at David, "THEN TELL HER NOT TO GET
IN MY FACE AGAIN! I WARNED HER!"

David screamed back. "GET OUT OF THIS FUCKING
HOUSE! OR I'M GOING TO KILL YOU!"

J.R. walked up close to David and yelled back, "YEAH,
YOU AND WHAT ARMY, ASSHOLE?"

I shouted, "J.R.! BACK OFF!"

By now, it looked like they would come to blows and then all of a sudden J.R. backed off.

He yelled, "YOU'RE ALL IDIOTS! I'M OUT OF HERE!"

After he left, I sat down at the kitchen table to find out exactly what had happened. Gina had an ice pack on her head and Valerie was sobbing uncontrollably.

I went to Valerie and hugged her tight as she cried.

"It's over now Val. I love you. Try to calm down."

David screamed, "I'M GONNA FUCKING KILL HIM! GET MY GUN!"

I yelled back, "KNOCK IT OFF DAVID! CALM DOWN! HE'S GONE!"

I started to get the story then from both of the girls as David paced around the kitchen, behind us.

I said, "When J.R. comes back, we are going to have a discussion. This behavior has to stop!"

David yelled, "I'M GONNA FUCKING KILL HIM. THAT WILL SETTLE EVERYTHING!"

Valerie yelled at him through her tears, "THAT'S NOT GOING TO SOLVE ANYTHING! FOR RIGHT NOW I JUST NEED YOUR SUPPORT! Can I just get a hug?"

She approached David for a hug. She walked right up to him, waiting for his arms to open and when he backed away from her and simply patted her on the back, she walked away from him abruptly. I could see that she was crushed. That was the last time that I ever heard her ask him for affection.

You can only get slapped in the face so many times before you just give up.

As he left the room, she said sarcastically "I don't really have a father at all, do I? What a joke."

Sometimes our hearts won't let us do what our minds tell us we should.

NO! We're married for life, for better or for worse.

I couldn't even entertain the thought of leaving the marriage. What kind of person would I be if I were to leave David in such dire straits emotionally? I had to take care of him. I had to try to help him. Wasn't that my responsibility?

David was so used to the extreme amount of hours at his gas station that one job now was not enough for him. So he took on a second job in security at the local discount store. I was glad that he was motivated but it left even less time for him to focus on himself and what he needed to do to be happy. He made no time for his family. He pretty much ignored us all, but thought that as long as he was handing me a paycheck that he was doing his part to take care of our family.

Everyone around us thought he was such a hard worker, such a good provider.

In reality, the money that he earned at the second job went right into his pocket for his own use. He used it for cigarettes and golf and going out with friends and whatever else he wanted. I'll admit that I went into his wallet many times to find that he had a couple of hundred dollars in there . . . sometimes more. It didn't matter if we had a shut off notice on our electric bill. I wouldn't dare take it! Oh no, that money was his to do with what he wanted. He was very clear about that. I tried to argue with him about it many times. It didn't matter. He didn't care. He handed me one paycheck and I was responsible for figuring out how to make it stretch.

His job in security was watching out for shoplifters. It wasn't long before I realized that he had become exactly that! It was such a joke really!

I remember the first time that I found him down in the basement with a pair of pliers trying to pull off the security tags from several items of clothing.

"What are you doing, David?" I asked him.

He smiled as he said, "What does it look like? I got these from the store for myself. They don't pay me nearly enough, so this kind of makes up for it!"

I shook my head back and forth and said, "Seriously . . . how can you do that?"

He turned his head towards me and said very matter of factly, "I do what I gotta do to take care of all of us here."

I sighed and said, "How do you sleep at night? How can you be so dishonest? What kind of example are you setting for your children?"

"Don't judge me," he said disgustedly, as he went back to his work there.

I just walked away.

I'm shocked at how dishonest you are. How can I possibly respect you at all? What you are doing is disgusting!

He would wrap stolen items for me as Christmas gifts, three of the same blouse in three different colors or sometimes the same color. I would open them and just look at him. I'd put them aside . . . never wore any of them.

I can't control what he does.

He couldn't figure out why I wasn't more grateful for the gifts he brought me. Couldn't I see that he was just trying to take care of his family by stealing things for us?

Unconscionable . . .

We used to go to a cottage in Wisconsin for a week at a time almost every summer. We would all be excited about going until we got there and David would get into one of his funks. It was inevitable. It happened every single time we went. So none of us was surprised, really. He'd scream and yell at all of us for no apparent reason. He would threaten that if the kids didn't do this or that, that he'd pack up the car early and we'd go home. During one of those vacations we received a phone call from our neighbor at home.

Mike said, "Karen, I hate to bother you while you are on vacation, but I figured you would want to know that something happened at your house here last night."

I said, "What's up? What happened, Mike?"

He replied, "Last night's weather here was really bad. Very violent rain storms . . . and apparently there was a micro-burst that went through our yards."

"Really?"

"Yes," Mike said. "And I wouldn't be bothering you if it weren't for your shed in your yard. For lack of a better way of saying this, it looks like it blew up. There's pieces of it all over your yard. I thought you'd want to know."

"Oh my," I said. "It must have been a bad one!"

"It was awful," Mike said. "For a while there, my wife and I and the kids were in our basement. I've never seen the sky look so ominous before."

"I appreciate the call, Mike. Thanks."

Mike asked, "Do you want me to clean up your yard for you?"

I replied, "Could you do that? That would be great! We won't be home until the day after tomorrow."

Mike said, "Sure, I can do that for you guys. No problem."

"Thanks so much, Mike. David's out in the boat now fishing but I'll tell him that you called. We will talk to you in a couple of days. Thanks again for calling."

In reality, while I was on the phone with Mike, David was sleeping. It was the middle of the day but he was in one of his funks. He stayed in bed all day to avoid us all . . . I guess.

When we got home, it was funny really. Mike had piled up all the pieces of the shed near the back of the house to keep all the pieces together. Every single nut and bolt had come undone and it seemed like every piece was there in the pile. Seemed like one of those freaky things of nature.

David and I had painstakingly put that shed together ourselves a couple of months before and I did not look forward to having to re-construct it with him. Working with David was like a nightmare every time. I tried to avoid it at all cost. Very often, any little household task became monumental when it came to David being a part of the repair. He would lose patience with any project and each one would often end up worse than when he had started.

I became quite the repair person myself . . . all I needed was a tool belt. It was so much easier to take care of things myself.

David decided that he was going to put that shed back together a couple of days after we returned home.

Oh, crap. Here we go . . .

David said, "I need your help. Come on outside in the yard."

Don't know why but I was always hopeful that things would go better this time than last.

"Okay, I'm coming," I said.

So off to the yard we went.

As we began to try to organize the pieces of the shed, I said, "Do you want to consider putting in some kind of foundation for this thing? Like they suggested in the original directions?"

"No, it doesn't need it," David replied.

"Okay," I said skeptically.

The pieces of the shed were made of hard plastic and because it had not been originally built on a level surface, almost all of the pieces were warped. It became more and more clear as we proceeded.

I held the pieces as we went while David tried to pry them together, forcing them into place. I shook my head as I realized that it was not going to work.

As he hammered at a bolt and hit his finger instead, he yelled. "MOTHER FUCKER! CAN YOU GET OVER HERE AND HELP ME?"

"I'm right here. What do you want me to do?" I asked.

JUST GET THE FUCK OVER HERE AND HOLD THIS! YOU'RE USELESS SOMETIMES!"

As I was holding a piece of the roof above me, two hours later, David said, "Can you move the fuck over? You're in my way!"

I could see that he was getting more and more annoyed; like a pressure cooker ready to explode, but I hung in there.

I replied, "I'm doing the best that I can here, David. This thing was not put together the right way the first time."

"FUCK YOU!" he said. "GIVE ME THAT HAMMER! I'LL GET IT DONE!"

"I think we might need another pair of hands here," I said.

He began to yell louder at me, "NO, WE DON'T! JUST GET THE FUCK OVER HERE AND HOLD THIS!"

As I tried to help him, he pushed me out of his way . . . hard.

I said, "I can't do this! I'll see if one of the kids will help you."

"STAY HERE BITCH! GOD DAMN IT! JUST HELP ME!"

By now, I figured the neighbors were going to hear us. I was feeling sick and disgusted as I walked away.

Tears began to sting my eyes as I said, "I can't do this!"

As I heard a loud thump behind me, I could see Gina walk towards me from the house quickly.

She ran over to the shed behind me to find that David had fallen to the floor. He was on his back, flailing around, like he was having some kind of attack.

I just watched as Gina stood over him and looked down at him and yelled, "DAD! ARE YOU OKAY?"

No response. Nothing. Still flailing . . .

This was not the first time that David had pretended to be having some kind of seizure.

She yelled louder this time, "DAD, WHAT'S WRONG WITH YOU?"

All of a sudden, his body went still, and he jumped to his feet.

I couldn't even look at him, his theatrics so outrageous.

Gina yelled at him again, "WHAT THE FUCK IS WRONG WITH YOU? DO YOU NEED TO GO TO THE HOSPITAL OR NOT! CUZ I'M TIRED OF WASTING MY TIME ON YOUR FUCKING GAMES!"

David brushed off his pants and looked at Gina and said, "I'm fine! I'm fine."

This was our ordinary . . .

❀-❀-❀

Even though he and I became more distant, I initiated sex occasionally with David. I would think to myself that it had been several months since the last time and I convinced myself that we still had a marriage if any type of intimacy occurred.

It was incredibly unfulfilling and disappointing, but I tried to convince myself that we were not just roommates.

He had no time for anything else but work. Along with the second job, he started going out every single Friday night with his work buddies.

I never did understand that.

I asked him, "Where are you going every Friday night?"

David answered, "I'm going out with my work buddies. We shoot some pool and eat and talk . . . that's it. No big deal."

I asked, "How many of you go out?"

He answered, "There's usually about ten of us."

I asked, "Doesn't anyone bring their spouse with them?"

He replied, "No, it's just the guys."

So he'd rush home from work every Friday night and jump in the shower. He wore nice clothes, combed his hair just right, and splashed on some cologne.

This is all for the guys?

I got a phone call from Nancy one Saturday morning.

She said, "Karen, I was out last night with some girlfriends at a dance club. My friend is getting married and we were there for her bachelorette party."

I said, "Did you have fun?"

Nancy said, "We had lots of fun but that's not why I'm calling you."

I replied, "Oh . . . what's up?"

"I hate to be the one to tell you this but if the situation were reversed, I'd want someone to tell me."

"What is it?" I asked with concern.

She said, "David was there. On the dance floor with some woman."

I said, "What? Are you lying?"

Nancy replied, "I wish I was, Karen. But he was having a great time dirty dancing with some woman."

"Did he see you?" I asked.

"He saw me, yes. I tapped him right on the shoulder and asked him what he was doing there."

"What the hell did he say?" I asked.

"He had a big smile on his face as he said he was dancing. He didn't look worried or anything. He was pretty cocky. Didn't even try to hide what he was doing or to make any excuse!"

I sighed and said, "I don't know what to say. I'm kind of dumbfounded."

Nancy said, "You're going to talk to him about it?"

"Of course, I'll have to," I said.

"I'm really sorry. Maybe I shouldn't have told you?" Nancy asked.

"No! I'm glad you did. I don't look forward to the confrontation with him," I answered.

Nancy said, "Well, you do with it whatever you need to Karen. I love you. Let me know if I can do anything to help, okay?"

"Okay, thanks Nancy," I replied.

When I hung up the phone, my eyes stung with tears and my mind was reeling with the information.

Hanging out with your guy friends, huh?

When he came home later that day, I confronted him.

"I talked to Nancy today. She told me that she saw you out at a club dancing with some woman last night! Can you explain that?"

David replied, "Yeah, I saw Nancy. It was no big deal. The woman I was dancing with works with me at the store."

I said incredulously, "What do you mean no big deal?"

I can't even believe your nerve!

"I told you that I go out with my work friends," said David. "She's just a girl that I work with. It didn't mean anything."

I said, "You told me that you go to a pizza bar, not a dance club!"

David replied, "We usually do. They changed their minds this time and went to the dance club instead. I just went along with the group."

"And you seriously don't see a problem with that?" I asked.

"YOU'RE MAKING A BIG DEAL ABOUT NOTHING! LEAVE ME ALONE!"

I was shocked by his arrogance.

You asshole. Who the fuck do you think you are?

I said, "IT IS A BIG DEAL! WOULD IT BE OKAY IF I DO THE SAME THING AND GO OUT DANCING WITH SOME GUY?"

He yelled at me then, "YOU BETTER NOT! IT WAS NO BIG DEAL! I WORK FUCKING HARD ALL WEEK AND I NEED TO GO OUT AND BLOW OFF SOME FUCKING STEAM! GET OVER IT ALREADY!"

That was it. No other explanation. He always justified his behavior. He never apologized, except when I begged him to. I thought that somehow I could move onto another day if he just said those words.

On occasion, to pacify me, he would blurt out, "OKAY! WHATEVER! I'M SORRY! GET OVER IT!"

You don't mean a word of it . . .

The Friday nights out never ended. I got to the point where I didn't really care what the hell he was doing. I was happy to have him out of the house. It was quieter. It was peaceful. I actually came to look forward to his being gone. The kids and I did our own things.

As religious as if he'd been a church goer, he was out every Friday night. Oftentimes he didn't return home until the wee hours of the morning on Saturday.

CHAPTER 21

A ND STILL MORE YEARS SLIPPED by . . .
One Friday night I got a phone call. I was watching TV
with J.R. He could see the look of shock on my face as I held
the phone to me ear.

The young woman on the phone said, "I'll have you know
that YOUR husband, and I use that word very lightly, is a
FUCKING MORON. He's been cheating on you with my
mother and he's been treating her like crap as well!"

I was speechless for a moment.

I said, "What? Who is this?"

She said, "You don't need to know my name but I'm telling
you loud and clear that your husband is cheating on you big
time with my mother!"

I said, "Who is your mother? What are you talking about?"

I could hear some confusion from the other end of the line.
I heard another woman's voice whispering, "What are you
doing? Are you crazy? This is none of your . . ." and with that
the line went dead.

I sat there dumbfounded with the cordless phone in my
hand. It felt like someone had punched me in the chest.

J.R. said, "Mom, are you okay? Who was that?"

I hesitated and said, "Uh . . . I don't know."

"What do you mean, Mom? I can tell you're upset. Tell me who that was."

I shook my head back and forth and tried to take a deep breath. I couldn't find the words.

Did I hear right?

J.R. said louder, "MOM, TELL ME WHAT'S WRONG!"

I said, "That was some woman. I don't know who it was. She said that her mother is having an affair with your dad."

"Oh . . . Mom," said J.R. "Do you believe her?"

I replied, "I don't know."

J.R. said, "Where is Dad right now? If this is true, I'd love to give him a piece of my mind!"

"It's Friday night. He's out with his friends."

J.R. asked, "Can you call him? He has his cell phone with him, doesn't he?"

"He always has it with him, yes. But I've tried to call him before when he's out on Friday nights and he never picks up."

J.R. was getting angry and he yelled, "I'M GOING TO CALL HIM RIGHT NOW! HE BETTER PICK UP!"

As J.R. dialed his number I just sat there on the couch. David did not pick up.

Sometimes our hearts won't let us do what our minds tell us we should.

David came home late that night. We had a discussion the following morning.

I said, "I got a phone call last night while you were out . . . from some young woman. She said that she was the daughter of some woman that you are seeing. What the hell is that about?"

Without batting an eyelash, he had an answer for me. He was just as calm as he could be.

David said, "That's strange."

"So who could it have been? Who would be calling me to tell me that?"

"I don't know but I'll find out for you. There must be some kind of explanation."

Seriously? That's all you have?

"I have to get to work now," David said. "But I'll look into this and see what I can find out."

Later that night, he had an answer for me. He'd had time to think about it.

He said, "So this security job where I'm working . . . there are a couple of women who work there and one of them got caught stealing last week. I was the one who caught her. I called the cops and she was arrested. I'm sure it had to be her daughter who called you. They are pissed off at me and want to get me into trouble with you."

"I'm supposed to believe that?" I asked.

He answered, "It's the truth. That's all there is to it." And he walked away.

I accepted the crap from David. I settled . . . It was easier than trying to think about how the hell to get out of the situation. No matter how many Al-Anon meetings I went to, I still did not have the courage to leave him. I was told at meetings that sometimes the best decision for the moment is no decision, that I would come to know the right one.

Will the answer EVER become clear to me?

I had to be patient with myself. It took a long time for my mind to become so muddled and confused with the disease of co-dependency. It would take a long time to be able to think more clearly.

And in reality I wanted to keep it together for the kids more than myself. I wanted to help them maintain some sense of normalcy . . . as warped as that may sound.

J.R. was in college now and the girls in high school. I dared to start to think about what my life would become once the kids were out on their own. It horrified me.

How can I live alone with him? He's bound to drag me down.

By now, the kids were so used to his crazed moods. It was our normal.

Gina and Valerie and I sat down for dinner in the kitchen. As I took the lasagna out of the oven, David joined us at the table without a word.

Gina said, "Dad, I'm having a problem with my car. I wonder if you'd have time to take a look at it for me."

No response.

"Dad, did you hear me?" asked Gina.

David hadn't showered yet from work. His hair was greasy. He reeked of the auto repair place that he worked at.

Gina looked at him and shook her head back and forth.

No response again.

David was looking down at the table. He did not acknowledge Gina's question or even her presence. It seemed as if he didn't even hear her. He started to rake his hands slowly through his dirty hair, over and over again. Along with that, his whole body started to shake as he then moved one hand to his chest.

As I brought the garlic bread to the table, I looked at him and walked back to the kitchen counter to get the knife. As I faced the kitchen sink, I shook my head back and forth and let out a huge sigh. I turned around then and leaned up against the kitchen counter and watched him.

This wasn't the first time. We never knew if we should take him seriously.

Gina asked, "Are you okay, Dad?"

No response.

Valerie looked at him and shook her head as she took a bite of her lasagna and said, "Mom, you've out done yourself again. This is delicious!"

"Thanks," I said.

Gina asked louder this time, "DAD! ARE YOU OKAY?"

No response.

Gina yelled louder, "DAD! DO I NEED TO CALL AN AMBULANCE? ARE YOU OKAY? YOU'RE PISSING ME OFF! ANSWER ME ALREADY!"

I walked over to him at the table then and poked him in the shoulder and said, "David, are you okay? Can you answer Gina?"

He jerked in his chair violently like I had hit him with a sledge hammer.

And like a caged animal he growled at me, "YOU BITCH, WHAT WAS THAT FOR?"

I stepped back a bit and said, "I just nudged you to get your attention. Answer your daughter."

He shook his head back and forth quickly as if to shake himself out of a trance and said, "What . . . what question? Who asked me a question?"

"I did," said Gina. "I asked you if you are okay. Why are you shaking that way and holding your chest? Are you having a heart attack? Should I call an ambulance?"

He moved his hands and placed them on the table and said, "No, I'm fine. I've just had a bad day."

Valerie quipped under her breath, "What else is new?"

"What did you ask me, Gina?" David asked.

"FIRST OF ALL, YOU HAVE TO STOP BEHAVING THAT WAY. ONE OF THESE DAYS YOU WILL REALLY BE HAVING A HEART ATTACK AND NONE OF US ARE GOING TO BELIEVE YOU! YOU'RE GOING TO FALL OVER AND DIE WHILE WE ALL WALK AWAY FROM YOU!" yelled Gina.

David yelled back now, "FUCK ALL OF YOU! I DON'T NEED THIS BULLSHIT!"

With that he stood up quickly, pushing his chair back with his legs so hard that it fell onto the floor. He picked up his plate full of food and walked over to the counter and dumped the whole plate inside the sink.

"FUCK YOU ALL!" he yelled as he stormed out of the room and up the stairs. I could hear the bedroom door slam behind him.

His behavior shook me up a bit, but for the most part we were all used to it.

As my heartbeat slowed to normal, I said quietly, "Gina, if you are having a problem with your car, we can take it to another mechanic. Apparently, your dad is just not capable of taking care of it for you."

Gina said, "YOU'D THINK I COULD COUNT ON HIM FOR SOMETHING? ANYTHING?"

I said, "I'm sorry that he pisses you off so much but it will be much easier to take it to someone else than to try to work with him."

"Whatever," said Gina.

"Let's just finish our dinner now, okay?"

Val said, "What time is your soccer game tomorrow, Gina? I want to be there for you."

The conversation between us returned to normal as soon as he was absent from the room.

Often times when the girls would treat David coldly, after one of his *episodes*, he'd blame me.

He'd yell at me, "YOU'RE TURNING THEM AGAINST ME! IT'S YOUR FAULT THAT THE GIRLS AREN'T TALKING TO ME! WHAT DID YOU TELL THEM?"

I'd reply, "ARE YOU KIDDING? YOU'VE CREATED YOUR OWN MISERY HERE! THEY ARE YOUNG ADULTS NOW WHO CAN MAKE UP THEIR OWN MINDS AND FORM THEIR OWN OPINIONS! I DON'T NEED TO TELL THEM ANYTHING! THAT'S ON YOU! YOU HAVE NO ONE TO BLAME BUT YOURSELF!"

He'd scream back, "FUCK YOU!"

This was my life . . .

By now, I'd gone back to working at a beauty salon a few days a week. I couldn't count on what David would provide. He had a hard time keeping a job for very long and was oftentimes *in between jobs.*

It felt great to be out working again. It felt good to make new friends and to keep up with the newest trends in hairstyling. It felt good to do something for me.

Sometimes I wonder if all the stress through those years contributed to the female issues that I started to experience. After two years and many visits to my doctor and to the hospital emergency room, it was decided that a hysterectomy might be the answer for me.

I remember walking out of the exam room and into the nurse's area where I was asked to have a seat to schedule the day and time for the procedure. Because of the excessive bleeding that I'd been experiencing, my hormones were surely out of control. I felt emotionally drained as I sat there and cried like a baby.

As I tried to calm myself enough to speak to the nurse, I assured her that my hormones were totally out of whack and that she did not need to call the psych ward for me.

The day before my surgery, I was more nervous than I'd ever been with anticipation. I was not feeling well physically or mentally. I was a total wreck.

I needed someone strong by my side to support me. I needed to be reassured that everything would be okay. I most certainly did not get anything that even resembled that from David.

In fact, he chose to mess with me at the very worst moment.

I was sitting on the edge of the couch staring at the TV but not watching the TV. Tears stung my eyes as I thought about all the things that could go wrong the next day in surgery.

David walked into the room and could very clearly see that I was upset.

He said, "Before you go to the hospital tomorrow, can you call the dentist for me and make an appointment for me? You're not going in until noon anyway."

I just looked at him with disbelief.

David asked me then, "Did you prepare plenty of meals for when you are in the hospital? Are they in the freezer?"

I stared at him for a moment without saying a word as the fury inside me looked for a way out. I felt like I might burst into pieces all over the room.

I stood up and I got up close to him. I looked him straight in the eyes as I screamed, "WHAT THE FUCK IS WRONG WITH YOU? CAN'T YOU SEE THAT I'M UPSET HERE? I'M TERRIFIED OF WHAT'S GOING TO

HAPPEN TO ME TOMORROW AND ALL YOU CAN THINK OF IS YOURSELF?"

He backed up a few steps away from me. He actually looked afraid of me. Can you imagine? It would have almost made me laugh . . . if I wasn't feeling so angry and out of control.

I could feel my face flush as I screamed, "DON'T YOU GIVE A FUCK ABOUT ME?"

He replied, "Well I . . . "

I didn't let him finish his thought.

"YOU ARE SUCH AN ASSHOLE. ALL YOU CARE ABOUT IS YOURSELF! I HATE YOU!"

For the first time in all the years we'd been together, I had the upper hand. I felt like a raging animal but I couldn't stop myself. The words came spewing out of my mouth uncontrollably . . . like vomit.

David dared to say, "Are you okay? You seem a bit crazy."

"I FEEL CRAZY! I'M SO SICK AND TIRED OF YOU! YOU DON'T GIVE A SHIT ABOUT ME! YOU NEVER HAVE!"

If I'd had a loaded gun in that moment, there's no doubt in my mind I would have shot him.

In all the years that we'd been married, I had never screamed at him this way with such abandon. I dared not to. In that moment though, it was like I was letting out all the rage that had been built up inside me for so many years.

He said, "Really, Karen, are you okay?"

"NO! I'M NOT! I'M SCARED TO DEATH! AND I CAN'T HANDLE YOUR BULLSHIT TODAY! I'M SICK OF IT! I'M SICK OF YOU!"

David said, "I'm sorry, Karen. What can I do?"

"NOTHING! JUST LEAVE ME ALONE! I CAN'T
STAND TO EVEN LOOK AT YOU!"

I grabbed my coat off of the coat rack, and grabbed my
keys off of the counter, and ran out to the garage. I jumped
into my car and slammed the door shut. I could see that David
had run out behind me. I could hardly see the ignition through
my tears but I managed to start the car and I screeched off
down the driveway and out into the street. I drove to the
nearby retail store and parked my car in the parking lot, away
from all the rest of the cars.

I sobbed inconsolably for what seemed like hours.

I was drained . . . physically and emotionally. It was one of
the lowest points in my life, but just for a moment.

As I reached into my purse for some tissues, I took some
deep breaths to try to calm down. As I did so my mind raced.
My life flashed before me. All the abuse that I'd endured over
the years came flooding into my memories.

My cell phone rang. It was him. I ignored it.

*Sometimes our hearts won't let us do what our minds tell
us we should.*

*Oh my God! Was he right? Was Keith right all those years
ago?*

What was happening to me? I'd never felt so out of control
in my life. I was totally losing myself in this marriage. I didn't
recognize myself anymore. I felt like I was on a life saver in the
middle of the ocean floating away slowly . . . all by myself.

And then all of a sudden, I knew. This was it! This was my
spiritual awakening . . . finally . . . it hit me.

I knew that we would have to part ways. I didn't have any
idea of exactly what that would look like and I couldn't
pinpoint exactly when it would happen but I knew that it was
coming.

I wasn't going to take it anymore! Not from anyone!
I decided at that moment.

I will be happy in this lifetime! I will get away. I will save myself. It's going to happen. I will be happy. Life is way too short to waste even a moment . . .

CONCLUSION

SOMETIMES OUR HEARTS WON'T LET us do what our minds tell us we should.

I still ask myself why I stayed so long. It's almost embarrassing now that I did. But I did the best I could with what I knew. There is a certain kind of paralysis that comes over you when you are subjected to long term abuse. It's a well-studied phenomenon. My self-esteem was shot. It was slowly chipped away from me by my abuser. It left deep debilitating scars. I had to find a safe plan to exit the situation I was in.

How did I finally get away? You can read all about it in my first book, *WORDS TO LOVE BY*. If you've already read it... you know!

I met a local newspaper columnist after I'd written *WORDS TO LOVE BY*. She wanted to do an article about me. When the article first came out, she titled it, "Putting It All Down on Paper." I attached the link for that story on my blog and when I checked it there, I saw that the title of the article had been changed for some reason. It now reads, "Writing Their Stories Can often Aid Abuse Victims in Their Healing."

As soon as I read that title, it made me feel uneasy. After all I'd been through, I had never admitted to being a victim of abuse.

I'd like to be known for my ability to write a compelling story though, not as a past victim of abuse, but I realize now that my past life led to the new.

As more time goes by, away from my abuser, I'm totally shocked when I think back to how I was living. It was so incredibly distorted.

In fact, I recently became aware of a psychological occurrence called Stockholm Syndrome, (SS). I was fascinated and horrified all at the same time as I learned more about it. I could relate to every aspect.

SS is named after a bank robbery that occurred in Stockholm, Sweden. Two bank robbers held four hostages, three women and one man, for six days. The hostages' lives were threatened as the captors negotiated with police. In fact, the hostages were strapped with dynamite for the majority of their captivity.

After the hostages were rescued, they exhibited a shocking attitude considering they were threatened, abused, and feared for their lives for over five days. In their media interviews, it was clear that they supported their captors and actually feared law enforcement personnel who came to their rescue. The hostages had begun to feel the captors were actually protecting them from the police. One woman later became engaged to one of the criminals and another developed a legal defense fund to aid in their criminal defense fees.

SS can be seen as a form of traumatic bonding, which does not necessarily require a hostage scenario, but which describes strong emotional ties that develop between two persons where one person intermittently harasses, beats, threatens, abuses, or intimidates the other. One commonly used hypothesis to explain the effect of SS is based on a Freudian theory. It suggests that the bonding is the individual's response to trauma in becoming a victim. Identifying with the aggressor is one way that the ego defends itself. When a victim believes the same values as the aggressor, they cease to be a threat.

There are several aspects of SS that can become apparent in abusive situations.

A *perceived threat* can be formed by direct, indirect, or witnessed methods. The abuser can directly threaten your life or their own. Their history of violence leads us to believe that they will carry out those threats. Witnessing a violent temper directed at a television, others on the highway, a third party or even the family dog, clearly sends us the message that we could be the next target of violence.

When an abuser shows the victim some *small kindness*, even though it is to the abuser's benefit as well, the victim interprets the small kindness as a positive trait. I can count many, many times when after David would rage at me and not talk to me for several days, his solution was to take me out to dinner. He thought that if he were doing that for me, that everything was forgiven and forgotten.

Abusers are often given *positive credit* for not abusing their partner, when the partner would have normally been subjected to verbal or physical abuse in a certain situation. I remember thinking . . . he never hit me directly, not on purpose anyway. He only spit in my face because he was so angry, right?

I can remember early in our relationship being on the golf course with him while he played. I thought it would be fun to drive the cart and to watch everyone golf. That was until he was not playing a very good game. He got angrier and angrier as he swore about how awful he was playing. And then he swung his club so hard at a ball with no particular destination in mind, with all his might. It hit me directly on the middle of my leg. I saw stars, it hurt so badly. He apologized for just a moment, blaming his bad game for the *accident.*

In abusive relationships, the victim has the sense they are always, 'walking on eggshells' . . . fearful of saying or doing anything that might prompt a violent or intimidating outburst. For their survival, they begin to see the world through the *abuser's perspective.* They begin to fix the things that might prompt an outburst, act in ways they know makes the abuser happy or avoid aspects of their own life that may prompt a problem. They become preoccupied with only the needs, desires, and habits of the abuser.

The abused person feels there is *no way to escape.* It's just not an option to leave. Many abusive relationships feel like til-death-do-us-part relationships . . . locked together by mutual financial issues, mutual intimate knowledge, or legal situations.

The abuser often locks their victim into the abusive relationship by making them feel *guilty.* Oftentimes the victim experiences a loss of self- esteem and self-confidence.

In SS, there is a daily preoccupation with *trouble.* The victim will clean the house, calm the children, scan the mail, avoid certain topics, and anticipate every issue of the abuser in an effort to avoid, trouble.

Okay, okay, so I was definitely a victim of abuse. There . . . I said it. The key word being, *was* ! NOT ANYMORE!

This is my *SECOND ACT.*

I live with my new husband now who is kind and generous and loving. I am still waiting for him to get angry with me. Anger from my partner was so much an everyday occurrence that I'm surprised with every day that goes by that my new husband doesn't get mad at me. I expect it to happen still, but am so happy that it hasn't.

The other day we were riding down the expressway and a car went by that had a luggage carrier on the roof. I had a flashback to the vacations that David and I, and the kids took to the cottage in the north woods of Wisconsin. Unfortunately the memories that came to mind were bad. I can remember how much work it was for me to pack up for that vacation when the kids were small. All the laundry had to be done, all the kids clothes packed, all the bedding had to be washed and packed. The meals for the week ahead had to be planned and then the car had to be packed. I did it all. When the week was over, it all had to be done again in reverse. When we arrived home after the eight hour ride, I walked into our house and opened up some windows and checked the answering machine for messages. The three kids were systematically carrying in all of the luggage and putting things in the rooms where they belonged. The coolers went in the kitchen, the dirty laundry down the stairs to the basement, the fishing gear downstairs, and the kid's clothes in each of their rooms.

I'll never forget the look on David's face as he walked up to the bedroom where I was. He said, "Why you lazy mother fucking bitch! Why aren't you helping us carry all this shit into the house?"

I said nothing. I was dumbfounded. Even I was surprised at his reaction. I shouldn't have been but I was. I didn't know what to say. Those are the kinds of memories I have from my thirty-two year marriage.

I have flashbacks occasionally. They used to be much more frequent. The strangest things sometime will trigger the thoughts that come rushing back.

I have this advice to others in hopeless circumstances.

Escaping from an emotionally abusive relationship is hard, but it will need to happen in order for you to be happy. Too many times women or men stay in these types of relationships because it is easier than leaving. The truth of the matter is no one deserves an unhappy and emotionally abusive relationship.

Spend some time reflecting on some of the things your abuser says and does to make you feel worthless and helpless. If your best friend did those things, would they still be your friend or would you replace them with a friend who treated you better? If you had an emotionally abusive friendship, you would walk away... that's human nature.

Stop trying to change the abuser and stop believing they will stop abusing you. Stop covering for them. Stop enabling them to continue doing what they're doing. Stop allowing them to control you. Stop thinking that they will change because abusers rarely change. They enjoy the power they have over you and others.

You may feel guilty after leaving but here's a cure for that. Remind yourselves of all the gory details of the past so that you may relish in the peaceful present. Remembering the bad times will make you feel incredibly grateful for the gift of serenity.

I can't believe after all these years just how emotional a journey writing *DARK SECRETS NO MORE* has been. In my research, I purchased a *used ONE DAY AT A TIME IN AL-ANON* book. I hadn't looked at it in years. I don't even know what happened to my original copy. The moment that it was in my hands again, I was overwhelmed with emotion.

I sobbed as the last thirty-five years flashed before me all the way to the present.

I started reading it and couldn't put it down. There was this huge ah-ha moment in realizing at that instant, just how much this book impacted my life when I needed it most. I also realized as I flipped through the pages just how many of its suggestions that I've put into practice in my life over the last thirty-five years, when I first stumbled upon Al-Anon.

I'd be remiss if I didn't say thank you to my Higher Power for giving me the serenity to accept the things that I cannot change, the courage to change the things that I can and the wisdom to know the difference.

It's so incredibly rewarding to know that because of these changes that I made in my life, even if it was only one little change at a time... that I've come to a place now where I feel like I do.

I've arrived. I am at the Zenith of my Life! Oh, what a GLORIOUS Feeling!

LETTER TO DAVID

I DO FORGIVE YOU, I needed to . . . for myself, but I will never forget.

The longer that I'm away from you, the more I realize just how incredibly dysfunctional my life with you had become. It shocks me to my core.

The only great result of our marriage is our children. They are such incredible young adults now. Each one of them is such a loving and productive part of this world. They are such success stories . . . despite your influence.

I don't think that even you would deny the fact that I was mother and father to all three of them . . . if you can be honest with yourself. You were never there for them emotionally. Because of your disease, you were not able.

All three are scarred for life because of the traumas you put them through. But with the proper guidance from many resources, they have all triumphed over their own admitted character flaws. They have each turned their negatives into positive parts of their lives. It's a miracle, really. The resilience shown by each of them is remarkable.

You had nothing to do with anything that is good about them.

Unlike you, our children are patient, and tolerant, and grateful. When you live for years in fear and doubt, you can't help but recognize every small blessing.

As for me, I relish my life now, every single moment of every single day. It is in remembering my horrible past that I can now enjoy even more, every peaceful moment of every day that I am blessed with. I am surrounded now with people who love and care for me. I wake with a smile every day in anticipation of what lies ahead.

No more fear . . .

ABOUT THE AUTHOR

KAREN L. BONCELA LIVES IN a suburb just outside of Chicago with her husband . . . her Knight in Shining Armor.

When she's not writing, she spends most of her time with her family. J.R. is a firefighter/paramedic, Gina is a nurse, and Valerie is a teacher. She has two grandchildren so far.

A mother couldn't be any prouder!

You can visit Karen's Blog at www.karenlboncela.com.
You can contact her at kared8111@hotmail.com.

Made in the USA
Lexington, KY
10 May 2015